T0277104

100 OF THE BEST

100 OF THE BEST

DARLINGTON'S GREATEST GAMES

PAUL HODGSON

First published by Pitch Publishing, 2022

Pitch Publishing
9 Donnington Park,
85 Birdham Road,
Chichester,
West Sussex,
PO20 7AJ
www.pitchpublishing.co.uk
info@pitchpublishing.co.uk

A CIP catalogue record is available for this book
from the British Library.

ISBN 978 1 80150 376 1

Typesetting and origination by Pitch Publishing
Printed and bound in Great Britain by TJ Books, Padstow

Contents

For my wife Jennifer, who is my
soulmate and best friend.

Acknowledgements

Thanks to Jane Camillin at Pitch Publishing for all her support and, as per usual, her patience – plus the editing team at Pitch. Thanks to my wife Jennifer for her never-ending patience and my PA Chris for his constant practical help. I'd like to say a massive thank you to all the Darlo fans for their support along the way, especially Ian Carter, Stephen Lowson, John Gray and Steve Keeney – all of whom feature in this book. In addition, I'd like to thank the following ex-Darlington players who through playing for the club have become firm friends: Mark Forster, Kevan Smith, Peter Kirkham, Simon Shaw, Craig Liddle, Robbie Painter, Paul Ward and Dale Anderson, as well as ex-Middlesbrough, Liverpool, Norwich and Sunderland striker but more importantly former Darlington manager David Hodgson, who kindly wrote the foreword for this book. I'm extremely grateful to him for this.

Finally, I'd like to express my sincere thanks to freelance writer Simon Weatherill and Craig Stoddart from the *Northern Echo* for allowing me to use some of their material. Last but no means least, I'm extremely grateful to current Darlington FC CEO David Johnston for the help and support he has given me with this, and indeed the many other projects I have undertaken since we met.

Foreword

By David Hodgson

In 2002/03 I was asked by Paul to write a few words as a foreword for his book, *When Push Comes to Shove*. I felt privileged at the time and now, almost 20 years later, I'm writing one for the second time, which I must admit made me feel very special.

Two things we have in common – the obvious, our names, and that we have a real love for Darlington Football Club. Our friendship is one that was cemented in 1997 at an away match at Barnet. Strange as it seems, it's engraved in my head step by step, or in Paul's case wheel by wheel.

Let me explain. Only 30 minutes into the game my eye was drawn to Paul slowly wheeling his way towards a steward. I literally watched every move as it happened. I could see him talking with the aforementioned steward, then the gate was opened. Next, he was on his way towards another steward, again after a two-minute chat he was on the home straight. One more steward to pass,

30 metres from me and the dugouts. I was still watching this scene unfold, while the game was going on, and then BOOM – he was next to me in the dugout.

'Hodgie, what the hell is going on?' he asked. I replied, 'Are you joking? We are destroying them with our possession.' Paul sat and thought for a few seconds before responding, 'But the objective of the game is to score or at least shoot.' There was no bad language, no abuse, just a simple remark that killed me. I then asked him, 'How the hell have you got all the way round the ground to get here?' Paul grinned before saying, 'I told them that I was your brother!'

From that day onwards, I admired his nerve and respect towards me as a manager and a friendship was sealed for life. I have two of his books in my collection and have read about the bigger projects he is producing and the awards and admiration that are coming his way. He is an extremely gifted man. He has disabilities which simply don't hold him back. But above all he is a true Darlo fan, one who I'm extremely proud to know.

David Hodgson

Introduction

Greatest games aren't always cup finals and title deciders, which, as a lifelong Darlington fan, is just as well as I would have been struggling to fill this book! But as any Darlo supporter will tell you, there has been plenty of drama and many unforgettable games.

Our memories as Quakers fans are filled with just as much drama and rollercoaster moments – our club more than most – and that is what I've tried to capture in this book. While most of the games you would expect to find in a collection such as this are indeed here, there are a few others that might evoke some raised eyebrows and a couple that might even raise the question, 'Why?'

There's a reason behind each one and while some may be more obvious than others, I hope you enjoy reading about one or two gems that might have otherwise been forgotten and confined to a stat in a history book. I reckon the next few years will probably yield another 20 or so new matches that could live happily in this book. However, here are 100 that should certainly stick in the memory banks for one reason or another. Enjoy the book and thanks for buying it.

Paul Hodgson

1

The 1970s

DARLINGTON V SOUTHPORT – 1972/73

The first Darlington game I ever saw was at a fog-shrouded Feethams on 6 January 1973 when I was only seven years old. Our visitors that day were Southport, who at the time were promotion contenders, while the Quakers were firmly rooted to the bottom of the Fourth Division.

Our home fixture against Workington on Boxing Day had already been postponed because a mixture of injuries and a flu epidemic had reduced Darlington to just eight fit players, and because of the foggy conditions the Southport game was only given the go-ahead by the referee an hour before kick-off.

Allan Jones, who had been sent on a three-week 'holiday' by the chairman, George Tait, had officially parted company with the football club on 21 December. He became the fourth Darlington manager to lose his job in only 15 months. His replacement was Ralph Brand.

The previous game, on 23 December 1972, had been away to Bradford City where we were hammered 7-0. Apparently, after the game at Valley Parade the newly installed Brand assured the press that the result had been a 'one-off' and that the team would never be beaten like that again.

Clearly he didn't believe, and neither did I, that lightning would strike twice.

Brand had an impressive pedigree as a player and knew all about scoring goals. Born in Edinburgh, he had played for Rangers, notching an impressive 206 goals in 317 games for the Ibrox club. He even ranks third among their postwar strikers, just behind Ally McCoist and Derek Johnstone.

However, the omens certainly didn't look good for the visit of Southport. On the day of the match, with only an hour to go before kick-off, Phil Owers, a 17-year-old rookie goalkeeper, was called upon to make his first-team debut in place of regular stopper Ernie Adams, who couldn't play due to injury.

The match was certainly a one-sided affair. By half-time the Quakers were 4-0 down and they went on to lose 7-0, which is their heaviest ever home league defeat to date. To cap it all, I'd pestered my mother for weeks on end to take me to a Darlington game. My abiding memory was, 'What have I come down here for in the middle of winter in the freezing cold?' Or words to that effect.

Throughout the game, as the avalanche of goals came thick and fast, much to the anger of some of the crowd, Brand remained in his seat in the directors' box instead of going down to the touchline to encourage his players. His semi-detached attitude to management was exemplified by the fact that he actually lived in Edinburgh where he was in business and only commuted to Darlington each Wednesday, when he remained until the following Saturday evening.

At the final whistle, the fans gave Phil a standing ovation. After all, he wasn't to blame for the rout. Had it not been for his bravery and agility, we might have eclipsed our heaviest ever league defeat when we lost 10-0 away to Doncaster on 25 January 1964.

As a matter of interest, Phil went on to carve out a lengthy career for himself and only retired in February 1999, still playing non-league football into his 50s, so that first appearance can't have been too traumatic!

Thinking about it, I bet that hasn't happened very often in professional football – two consecutive 7-0 defeats with two different goalkeepers. Those two results must have struck a chord with David Frost, who in February of that year highlighted our plight by making a documentary about the club for ITV.

At the end of that season, which saw Southport crowned as champions of the old Fourth Division, Brand's men finished bottom and had to apply yet again for re-election at the Football League Annual General Meeting in June 1973. Thankfully, we managed to retain our status with a majority of 12 votes over our nearest rivals, Yeovil Town. Darlington polled only 26 votes (the lowest successful total since the war) and were perhaps fortunate that the non-league clubs that they were up against were competing with each other and had split the vote (Yeovil polled 14 votes, Kettering 12 and Wigan Athletic ten). Had the non-league applicants been better organised and hadn't put forward more than one candidate, Darlington's application may not have been successful.

Trust me to start supporting the club during our worst ever season in the Football League. Out of 46 league games, Darlington won only seven, which was one fewer than our previous worst in 1936/37. So, after such a dismal introduction to life as a Darlo fan, why did I go back for more? Over the years I have often thought about that. Could it have been the smell of Bovril or pork pies, wafting towards me from the refreshment kiosk, which indelibly imprinted themselves on my consciousness? Perhaps I was eagerly awaiting the sound of an air horn to bring the team and the crowd to life. Maybe, though, it was the devoted fans standing on the North Terrace who captivated me, drumming out that incessant 11-beat pattern, like a Morse Code message, on the resonant fabric of the so-called Tin Shed – dah, dah / dah, dah, dah / dah, dah, dah, dah / Darlo.

Surely it can't have been the quality of the football on offer at the time that enthralled me. During the 1970s the

Quakers were well and truly anchored in the doldrums and had to make five re-election applications in just 11 seasons. Was I therefore simply a glutton for punishment? I suppose I must have thought, as football fans generally do when their team is faring badly, that things could only get better. And in that respect I was right.

DARLINGTON V SCUNTHORPE UNITED – 1973/74

Dick Connor was appointed manager of Darlington in the summer of 1973 following the ever-elusive Ralph Brand's departure. Connor had the unenviable task of reversing the fortunes of the Quakers, who had just suffered their worst season ever. Supporters voted with their feet and the average Feethams attendance was 1,697, the lowest in the club's history.

The 1973/74 season became another long struggle to stay away from the bottom positions in the league table. The team only scored nine goals in its first 15 league games and it was 10 November before they managed twice in one game. The shortage of goals wasn't helped when the previous season's top scorer, Peter Graham, was sold to Lincoln City at the end of September.

Darlington only managed five wins in their first 28 games and not surprisingly found themselves second from bottom in the table at the end of January. Their next opponents at Feethams would be Scunthorpe United on 3 February. Darlington had 20 points and Scunthorpe were four better off but had a dreadful away record of one win and one draw from 12 games, so the hosts saw it as a great opportunity to grab two points. Connor had recently strengthened his defence with a double signing from Rochdale. Centre-half Colin Blant and left-back Dick Renwick would both be making their third appearances for the club. Midfielder Gordon Cattrell and striker Bill Atkins would both miss the game through injury. Their places went to Norman Lees and Billy Yeats.

Away from football, the winter of 1973/74 became known as 'The Winter of Discontent', a time of power cuts and the three-day week. Games under floodlights were banned because of electricity shortages, so football experimented with Sunday games for the first time and Darlington switched four home matches to Sundays. Scunthorpe would be the second of these. The previous weekend had seen the Quakers play two home games, against Stockport (1-1) on the Saturday and against Torquay United (0-0) on the Sunday. The experiment with Sunday football virtually doubled the attendance, from 1,533 on the Saturday compared to 3,054 the following day. Darlington were hoping for another good crowd against Scunthorpe, a game that I attended with my mother.

The club's hopes were realised as another healthy crowd of 3,006 turned out for the 2.15pm kick-off. They saw Darlo make a strong start and control the game from start to finish. Visiting keeper Geoff Barnard was in fine form and single-handedly kept the home side at bay. In the early stages he punched a goalbound Colin Blant header over the bar, scrambled to smother a deflected Steve Holbrook shot and then parried well from a Colin Sinclair piledriver. The visitors simply couldn't deal with the strong running and pace of Don Burluraux and Sinclair. A goal had to come and the only surprise was that it took until the 39th minute to arrive. A long cross by Dick Renwick just evaded the best efforts of Yeats at the near post, but Burluraux met it at the far post and slid it past Barnard. I can remember being an excited little boy as my mother fed me my Bovril and pork pie at half-time.

The one-way traffic continued in the second half with Quakers goalkeeper Gordon Morritt a virtual spectator. Billy Horner had a shot cleared off the line by United full-back Barry Lynch, and then Yeats just failed to connect with another great Renwick cross. The home side lost Holbrook with a knee injury on 59 minutes but, if anything, that strengthened Darlo as substitute Alan Duffy took control of the midfield and started spraying passes around. One superb cross to the far post was met by Yeats but he headed narrowly wide into the side netting. Then, in the 65th minute, Duffy played a long, raking pass into the path of Sinclair who was brought down by Chris Simpkin as he broke into the box. Gordon Jones stroked home the penalty.

Darlington continued to look for more goals. Burluraux cracked in a stinging drive that Barnard did well to hold, and then Sinclair hit a shot on the turn that went just wide. Duffy smashed a 20-yarder that went just over the bar, then Barnard made a brilliant reflex save from a point-blank Sinclair header. Dick Connor's men completed the scoring in the final minute. The hard-working Yeats created an opening for Norman Lees who burst through and smashed a shot in off the post from just outside the box. I hugged my mother when that goal went in, I couldn't talk very much at that time. That didn't seem to matter that day as I'm sure that the huge smile on my face explained to her how happy I was!

The 3-0 win lifted Darlington two places in the table and raised hopes of escaping the dreaded bottom four. They left it late though. A 4-2 win at home to Barnsley on the last day of the season (another game that I attended with my mother) ensured that they finished fifth from bottom, one point clear of Crewe Alexandra.

SHEFFIELD WEDNESDAY V DARLINGTON – 1975/76

The summer of 1975 supplied fans of Darlington Football Club with even more drama and upheaval than normal. The Quakers had finished the 1974/75 season in 21st place and so again had to apply for re-election, along with Swansea, Workington and Scunthorpe United. All four clubs successfully retained their league status at the AGM at the beginning of June. Three days later, manager Billy Horner, who had replaced Dick Connor, left to become a coach at Hartlepool United. He'd had a long-running battle with chairman George Tait and cited 'a clash of personalities' as his reason for resigning. 'It is in the club's best interests that I leave,' he said at the time.

Horner was the seventh manager to have resigned or be sacked during Tait's four-year reign as chairman. In those four years, the club had never finished in the top half of the table, had never got beyond the second round of any cup competition, the reserve team had been disbanded and there was not a single apprentice player on the staff.

Things looked bleak, and at a stormy board meeting the following week Tait retained control of the club and appointed coach Peter Madden as the new manager. Madden immediately started strengthening the playing squad and preparing for the new season. He signed former Manchester City goalkeeper Alan Ogley from Stockport, defenders Bobby Noble from Southport and Jimmy Cochrane from Middlesbrough, midfielder Dave Crosson from Newcastle and striker Eddie Rowles from Torquay United. Pre-season preparations went well, and the team were actually unbeaten in their six friendly matches. With this in mind, everyone was in confident mood as the first day of the season drew near.

Darlington began their season with a 2-0 home win over Scunthorpe United, and then switched their attention to the League Cup. They had been paired with Sheffield Wednesday in the two-legged first round.

Wednesday had been relegated from the Second Division in the previous season and were tipped by many to make an immediate return. A crowd of 3,581 was at Feethams for the first leg to see Wednesday grab a fortunate 2-0 win with late goals by Mick Prendergast and Eric Potts.

The Quakers had fought well and more than held their own, but few people gave them much hope for the following week's second leg. In between the two cup ties, Darlington travelled down to Bournemouth for a league game and came away with a 2-1 win, so it was a confident group of players who set out for Hillsborough on 27 August. I couldn't go to this match. However, Simon Weatherill kindly supplied me with the following match report:

'Manager Peter Madden made changes for the trip to Sheffield. Club captain Colin Blant had served a three-match suspension and came back into the team for his first appearance of the season. He replaced Norman Lees, who in turn had played in place of the injured Bobby Noble at Bournemouth. The previous season's top scorer, Stan Webb, missed out with damaged ankle ligaments and his place went to the fit-again Colin Sinclair, who'd missed the last two games with a thigh injury. Wednesday would be without England international Colin Harvey, who had a thigh strain. His place went to Ken Knighton, who, as a matter of interest, later went on to manage Sunderland.

'A crowd of 7,452 were at Hillsborough to see both sides make a bright opening. Darlington almost struck first in the fifth minute when a fierce shot by Steve Holbrook brought home keeper Neil Ramsbottom to his knees. Wednesday hit back, and Quakers keeper Alan Ogley had to be at his best to keep out Phil Henson after he had been put clear by Eric Potts. Then Brian Joicey was brilliantly denied when Ogley went full-length, diving at his feet. Wednesday's main threat was tricky right-winger Potts, but once Jimmy Cochrane had got to grips with him, the Quakers began to take control of the game. Their best chance of the half fell to Colin Blant but he headed over from five yards out after running on to Cochrane's floated free kick.

'Peter Madden's men grabbed the lead five minutes into the second half. Steve Holbrook robbed home full-back Jimmy Quinn. He moved into the area while holding the defender off and fired an unstoppable shot into the roof of the net from an acute angle, giving Ramsbottom no chance. Things got even better for Darlington ten minutes later when Colin Sinclair added a second. Former Manchester United midfielder Eric Young won the ball in midfield and advanced towards goal before sliding the ball to Sinclair. His first time shot from the edge of the box screamed past Ramsbottom into the net. The keeper got a hand to it but couldn't keep it out.

'Wednesday then had their best spell of the game as they searched for the goal that would put them through, but the Darlington defence held firm with Ogley in particular in superb form. He saved well from a Mick

Prendergast shot and a Dave Herbert header and then Cochrane headed off the line to keep Henson out. In the closing minutes Joicey put in a dangerous-looking header that just cleared the bar, but the Quakers held on for a famous 2-0 victory.

'The only bad news on the night came after the game when Madden lost the toss to decide the venue of the replay, so Darlington would have to travel to Hillsborough again on the following Wednesday.'

In between their two trips to Sheffield, Peter Madden's men beat Elton John's Watford 1-0 at Feethams (a game that I again attended with my mother) to take them to the top of the Fourth Division with a 100 per cent record. Three wins out of three; their best start to a league campaign since 1948.

The replay at Hillsborough on 3 September brought even more good news. After playing out a goalless draw in front of a crowd of 6,276, the Quakers won the penalty shoot-out to advance into round two. They successfully converted all five of their penalties through Colin Sinclair, Jimmy Cochrane, Stan Webb, Alec Smith and Eric Young, while for Wednesday Mick Prendergast fired wide and Ogley saved from Danny Cameron. Darlington's reward was a home tie against Luton Town, who were beaten 2-1 with two Stan Webb goals in front of a crowd of 6,601. This earned them a third-round tie at Upton Park, where West Ham proved too strong for Darlo and ended their excellent cup run with a 3-0 victory.

DARLINGTON V SWANSEA CITY – 1975/76

When I started supporting Darlo during the 1970s, apart from a few good cup runs, we were invariably struggling to avoid finishing in the bottom four. At the time I thought this was the norm.

With me being at boarding school during the week (up until this match) I could only go to the odd Saturday fixture; even so, it wasn't long before some of the players began to recognise me and came over for a chat prior to the kick-off. I can remember that Clive Nattress, Steve Holbrook and Colin Sinclair did this fairly regularly.

Nattress was a free transfer signing from Blackpool and played at right-back until he moved to Halifax Town in 1979, before returning to the club in 1986 for a short stint.

Holbrook joined Darlo in 1970 from Hull City and the speedy right-winger ended up playing over 100 games for the club, before eventually signing for Gateshead in 1977.

Sinclair was signed from Raith Rovers for a small fee – anywhere between £3,000 and £5,000, depending on whether you believe the club's accounts or Colin's version of events. This is how the man himself describes the fateful moment that he signed for Darlo, 'The deal was done at Newcastle Railway Station and there were a few brown envelopes handed about. One came my way with £500 in it.' He went on to score 65 goals in 223 appearances for the Quakers before he was eventually transferred to Hereford United in 1976 for a fee in the region of £15,000.

Anyway, back to the game in question, our last of the season, against Swansea City, a match that I attended with my mother, despite it being midweek. I skived school, don't tell anyone! Darlo needed a point to avoid re-election. Stan Webb scored for the home team in the 65th minute and Swansea equalised in the 85th through Alan Curtis.

The celebrations after the final whistle were unbelievable. The players were dancing on the pitch and the fans were singing, 'We are the champions.' The club had achieved their aim of not finishing in the bottom four and therefore not having to apply for re-election. That sadly was the limit of their ambition.

Nowadays, a manager would be sacked if his team finished fifth from bottom of the table. How times change.

DARLINGTON V WIMBLEDON – 1977/78

The first half of the 1970s was not a good time to be a Darlington fan: three applications for re-election (plus another three near misses), nine managers, dwindling crowds and a constant fight for survival on the financial front. By the 1977/78 season though, Peter Madden had at last introduced some stability and hope to the club. As mentioned earlier in this chapter, he'd taken over the managerial post in the summer of 1975, so was in his third season at the helm. In the previous season he'd led the team to a creditable 11th place in the league, their best finish for seven years, and so hopes were high that he could take Darlo to an even better result in the new campaign. He would have to do it with a wafer-thin squad though as finances dictated that he run a tight ship. They started the new season with a squad of only 15 players and still with no reserve or youth team, the club had no pool of players to call on in an emergency and so the team quite often picked itself, and players often had to turn out, even when not fully fit.

Initially, this didn't seem to affect the team too much. After a dodgy start, with three defeats and a draw from their first four league games, things improved and a run of just one defeat in the next ten games lifted Darlo into a comfortable mid-table position. By the time Wimbledon visited Feethams on 29 October, the Quakers sat in 14th place in the Fourth Division table with 14 points from 14 games.

Wimbledon would be making their first ever visit to Feethams after being elected to the Football League in the previous summer, at the expense of Workington. The Dons had won three successive Southern League titles and enjoyed some FA Cup success with high-profile games against Burnley, Leeds United and Middlesbrough prior to eventually winning their Football League place. Workington had been making their fourth successive re-election application, so it was perhaps no surprise when the clubs had swapped places. Wimbledon had struggled with their early season form and travelled to the north-east four places and three points worse off than their hosts. Darlington were on a six-match unbeaten run and with injuries to goalkeeper Martin Burleigh (now sadly no longer with us), midfielder Eric Young and winger Lloyd Maitland, the team virtually picked itself so manager Madden had no hesitation in naming an unchanged side.

A crowd of 2,710 were at Feethams for the Saturday afternoon fixture; my mother and I were among them. We saw the home side very nearly take the lead in only the second minute when centre-forward Ron Ferguson (one of my favourite players from the 1970s) cut in from the right and drove a low cross/shot into the goalmouth. Dons defender Dave Donaldson deflected the ball and it seemed to be sneaking just inside the far post before keeper Richard Teale launched himself full-length and clawed it wide.

The game then developed into a scrappy, hard-fought stalemate with chances at a premium. This was eventually broken in the 30th minute with a spectacular strike by Neil Hague. Barry Lyons intercepted a clearance and made progress down the right. His cross into the box was headed wide by Dons centre-half Billy Edwards. From the resultant corner Jimmy Seal headed towards goal but it was hacked clear by full-back Dave Galvin. The clearance fell perfectly for Hague who smashed a left-footed volley into the top corner from 30 yards out with Teale absolutely helpless.

Wimbledon scored a shock equaliser a minute before half-time when the ball bounced awkwardly in the Darlington penalty area and referee Mike Peck ruled that John Stone had handled. Billy Holmes stepped up to send Phil Owers the wrong way from the spot.

The second half began with the home side on top and they almost regained the lead when Eddie Rowles broke clear down the right and squared the ball into the middle where Lyons volleyed just over. The Quakers were back in front after 58 minutes. Jimmy Cochrane played a short free kick to Stone whose deep cross to the far post was missed by Steve Galliers but met by Clive Nattress. He completely mishit his shot from an acute angle but the ball bobbled across the goalmouth and into the net just inside the far post. The visitors tried to respond and went close to an equaliser when Owers misjudged a left-wing corner, but Derek Craig was on hand to head the ball out for another corner from underneath his own crossbar.

Darlington made the game safe in the 81st minute with another controversial penalty decision by Mr Peck. Ferguson went down just inside the box after an innocuous-looking challenge by Edwards. Mr Peck thought it worthy of a penalty and Dennis Wann sent Teale the wrong way from the spot. I can remember leaving the ground with my mother thinking that we could gain promotion. Looking back, I was being very optimistic.

The 3-1 win lifted Darlo up to 11th place in the table but inconsistent results meant that they failed to improve their position any further. Their season was further hampered by the sale of top scorer Eddie Rowles to Colchester United for £15,000 in December 1977. They continued to struggle along with their tiny squad and eventually finished 19th with 41 points, only securing safety from the bottom four with one game to spare. Interestingly, Peter Madden only used 17 players throughout the whole season. This included Chris Jones (who was signed on loan from Doncaster Rovers to replace Rowles) and player-coach Len Walker who had to step in and play as an emergency centre-half for two games at the end of the season when the club was down to ten fit players. Rowles finished the season as joint top scorer, with Dennis Wann, even though he left after 21 league games.

DARLINGTON V FULHAM – LEAGUE CUP SECOND-ROUND REPLAY 1978/79

The 1978/79 campaign would see Peter Madden begin his fourth season as manager – quite an achievement in the unpredictable world of Darlington Football Club in the 1970s. Things started promisingly in the League Cup with a victory over Mansfield Town in the first round.

Their league form was less impressive though and one win from the first six games, with only two goals scored, meant that the Quakers were already struggling at the wrong end of the table.

Madden had identified the need for a centre-forward and spent the summer and the early weeks of the season trying to recruit the man he wanted. He made a £15,000 bid for Terry Eccles from Huddersfield Town, then a £16,000 bid to Cambridge United for Sammy Morgan, but both players chose to try their luck abroad. Madden then made an incredible £35,000 offer for long-term target Joe Cooke from Bradford City but that was rejected. The breakthrough in the transfer market came in October when Madden paid Middlesbrough £20,000 for Alan Walsh (I'm still in contact with 'Walshy' to this day). At that time, that was a lot of money and quite a risk, to spend that kind of money on a 21-year-old with only three substitute appearances for the Boro.

Once again I skived off school to go to this midweek League Cup second-round replay at home to Fulham with my mother. Thinking about it, not many mothers would let their child stay off school to attend a football match. I was very lucky that mine did, more than once!

Having drawn 2-2 at Craven Cottage, with Derek Craig and Dennis Wann scoring our goals, I can remember entering my beloved Feethams in the pouring rain eagerly anticipating the match.

As my mother and I sat in the East Stand paddock watching the match against a team who were two leagues above us, I can remember thinking that the rain was proving to be a leveller and it came as no surprise to me when the score was 0-0 at the interval.

However, that changed in the 63rd minute when Barry Lyons, the former Nottingham Forest star, got the only goal of the game from the penalty spot after Terry Bullivant and Kevin Lock combined to bring down our speedy right-winger, Lloyd Maitland, to earn his team a plum third-round tie away at First Division Everton.

I can remember being overjoyed as my mother and I ventured home in the still pouring rain.

EVERTON V DARLINGTON – LEAGUE CUP THIRD ROUND 1978/79

Unfortunately, I couldn't go to the Everton match because I was at boarding school at the time. However, I can remember being glued to the radio in my bedroom listening to the game. Here's what I recall. It goes without saying that I have checked the facts using an old match report, kindly supplied by Simon Weatherill, given that I was a child at the time the match was played.

As I listened to the radio, I quickly realised that Darlington had packed their defence and in the early stages easily snuffed out the home team's forwards, Bob Latchford and Mick Walsh. However, they missed a golden opportunity in the 16th minute when Jimmy

Cochrane's free kick from the left was headed down by centre-half Derek Craig to striker Jimmy Seal, who miscued his shot from six yards and the ball ended up in the arms of an extremely grateful Everton goalkeeper George Wood and the chance was gone. The home side came more into the game and Darlington keeper Martin Burleigh made a brilliant save from Andy King in the 37th minute. The visitors continued to cause their First Division opponents problems and just before the interval, goalkeeper Wood grabbed the ball off John Stone's head, following an excellent free kick from Quakers winger Dennis Wann.

Burleigh was the first keeper to make a save of any worth in the second half when in the 54th minute he dived full-length to keep out a rasping 20-yard drive from Geoff Nulty. Shortly after, the home side took the lead. Colin Todd (later to manage Darlington) crossed, King flicked it on and midfielder Martin Dobson slotted the ball home. Not long after his goal, Dobson thought that he'd doubled his side's lead when he put the ball in the net following a weak back pass from defender Clive Nattress, but the goal was chalked off for offside. Just prior to that, Stone had blasted a free kick wide for Darlington after Lloyd Maitland had been brought down by Nulty 30 yards out.

The Quakers continued to press and in the 60th minute Wann put another 30-yard free kick inches wide with Wood well beaten. Later in the game, Wood was in trouble again when he handled outside the box. Unfortunately for the visitors, captain Barry Lyons blasted the free kick just wide of the post with Wood again struggling. In the final ten minutes, Peter Madden's men laid siege to the Everton goal but the home team held out to ensure their somewhat lucky passage into the fourth round.

As I switched my radio off, I can remember thinking that I was proud of my team and wished I'd been there to witness such a brilliant Darlington performance.

DARLINGTON V PORT VALE – 1978/79

Alan Walsh made his debut at Rochdale on 21 October 1978. The game ended in a 2-1 defeat and proved to be Madden's last in charge. Madden was asked to resign and was replaced by player-coach Len Walker. One of Madden's final acts had been to secure the signing of Walsh, who would go on to become a Darlo legend and their joint-highest goalscorer of all time. I was disappointed that Madden left, as I had always liked him.

Walker took over the reins with the club deep in re-election trouble. They sat third from bottom in the Fourth Division with three wins and ten points from their 14 games. It was a difficult first week for Walker with Madden's 'resignation' leaving Darlo in turmoil, with several players in open revolt. Former Newcastle United goalkeeper Martin Burleigh, Eric Probert and top scorer John Stone openly stated that they were only at the club because of Madden and were now considering their futures. Walsh must have wondered what he had walked into.

Walker's first game in charge, and Walsh's home debut, would be against Port Vale on 28 October (yet again, my mother accompanied me). Our visitors were doing slightly better than their hosts and sat in 16th place, three points better off. They had one of the better away records in the division with four victories on the road. So, with this in mind, this fixture would provide a stiff test for the Quakers.

Things had calmed down slightly at Feethams by the time Saturday came around. After an appeal by Madden for the players to rally together, Walker was able to announce an unchanged 11 for the visit of Vale. His options were limited as he was still without the experienced midfield pairing of Barry Lyons and Eric Probert through injury. Derek Craig had been doubtful, but he recovered from knee and thigh injuries to keep his place in the side.

Only 1,793 people turned out to see the first game of the Len Walker era. In brilliant sunshine, my mother and I witnessed an even start to the game with early chances created at both ends. Alan Walsh and Dennis Wann combined to send Ron Ferguson away down the left. He beat Gerry Keenan and found Jimmy Seal but his tame shot was easily saved by visiting keeper John

Connaughton. Bernie Wright and Keenan went close for Vale before Felix Healey brought a good save out of Martin Burleigh. Darlington hit back and a clever overhead kick by Lloyd Maitland very nearly caught Connaughton out, but he managed to palm the ball away and it was scrambled to safety.

The home side took the lead in the 17th minute with a superb goal by Walsh, who immediately endeared himself to the home fans. Full-back Jimmy Cochrane cleverly broke up an attack and found Walsh in space near the halfway line. He showed deceptive pace as he ran fully 30 yards with the ball, leaving the Vale defenders in his wake, before coolly firing past the helpless keeper from the edge of the box. The Quakers were now fully on top as they threatened to double their lead before half-time with Ferguson twice going close. In the 40th minute he sent a header just over the top and then on the stroke of half-time, he latched on to a Derek Craig knock-down in front of goal, but the Vale defence scrambled the ball clear before he could get a shot away.

The second half began with the visitors on top and looking likely to get back into the game. They failed to make the pressure count though and Darlo increased their lead in the 67th minute. Ferguson was fouled 25 yards out by Graham Hawkins. John Stone rolled a short free kick to Seal who blasted home with a left-footed drive. Seal almost made it 3-0 a minute later but his shot was fractionally off target.

The home fans didn't have to wait long for a third goal though and it duly arrived in the 70th minute. Walsh tormented the Vale defence down the left wing before unselfishly squaring the ball to Ferguson who fired home. The visitors briefly threatened when Healey fired at goal which produced a magnificent fingertip save from Burleigh, but any hopes they had of getting back into the game were ended on 79 minutes when Ken Todd was sent off. He'd been booked a minute earlier for a foul on Ferguson, then he retaliated when he himself was fouled by Wann and the referee had no hesitation in sending him off.

Seal completed the victory with the fourth goal in the last minute. Again, it was Walsh supplying the ammunition with a long cross to the far post that was headed down by Stone and tapped in by Seal from a couple of yards out. While being overjoyed with the victory, I can remember thinking that the club had been very hasty in letting Peter Madden go.

The 4-0 win briefly lifted the Quakers out of the bottom four, something that I was relieved about at the time.

DARLINGTON V ALDERSHOT – 1978/79

Under new manager Len Walker, Darlington's results improved very slightly and they managed to keep themselves above the re-election zone. However, three consecutive home defeats in March dropped them back into the bottom four. Walker strengthened the squad by signing striker John Peachey from Barnsley for £7,000 and securing midfielder Graeme Hedley on a month's loan from Middlesbrough.

Walker welcomed some old friends to Feethams when Aldershot visited on 3 April (yet another game that my ever-loyal mother took me to). He'd made a club record 450 appearances for the Shots in a 14-year association career there which had ended when he'd moved to Darlington as Peter Madden's assistant. Aldershot were flying high in the division and were pushing hard for promotion. They were sat in third place, only three points off the top, and would provide a difficult test. Darlington had injury problems for the game. Top scorer John Stone was missing with a groin strain and Neil Hague was also absent after being involved in a car crash earlier in the day. Hedley made his home debut and Dave Crosson stepped into central defence to replace Hague.

A disappointing crowd of only 1,267 braved the horrible weather to see Darlington make a bright start to the game. They could and indeed should have taken the lead in the eighth minute when a deep Dennis Wann corner was headed back across goal by Derek Craig but John Peachey headed straight at visiting keeper Glen Johnson from only a couple of yards out. It proved a costly miss as the Shots went straight down the other end and opened the scoring. A long ball forward was flicked on by John Dungworth, and Andy Needham outpaced the home defence and tucked the ball neatly past Martin Burleigh. Darlington continued to press forward, prompted by Hedley who was running the midfield, and Alan Walsh who was continually testing Johnson in the visitors' goal with a string of shots and crosses with no reward.

The best chance fell to Peachey again when Johnson parried a Walsh shot but the centre-forward lifted his shot over the bar from 12 yards out. Hedley almost equalised just before half-time but his clever lob was brilliantly saved by the agile Johnson.

The one-way traffic continued in the second half with Aldershot only threatening occasionally on the counter-attack. Walsh drove a fierce 35-yard free kick just wide and then Dave Crosson moved up from the back to hit a scorching 30-yard blockbuster but he was denied by another acrobatic Johnson save. Just when it seemed as if the home side were beginning to run out of steam, the pressure paid off and they equalised in the 69th minute. Hedley was fouled 25 yards from goal. Walsh's fierce free kick was parried by Johnson but this time Peachey was on hand to fire home the loose ball.

Six minutes later the home side were in front, from yet another free kick. Dennis Wann was fouled out wide on the left. He picked himself up and curled in the free kick that was headed powerfully home by Peachey from ten yards out. Darlo continued to press forward and almost added a third when Ron Ferguson headed narrowly wide from a Hedley cross. Darlington had put in their best performance for months and thoroughly deserved the two points. The man of the match was Peachey for his two goals, but he was ably assisted by Hedley, who dominated the midfield and Walsh who had been a constant threat going forward. I left the ground hopeful that Darlington would avoid re-election.

However, it wasn't to be, as a poor end to the season with two wins from the last 12 games sealed their fate and they finished in 21st place and had to apply for re-election, along with Doncaster Rovers, Halifax Town and Crewe Alexandra. The poor finish cost Walker his job. He was sacked in the summer and replaced by Billy Elliott. Luckily, they polled enough votes to retain our league status. This left me a very relieved young man.

2

The 1980s

DARLINGTON V NORTHAMPTON TOWN
– 1980/81

The first game of a brand-new season is always a time of great optimism. Everyone starting on zero points and feeling that this year could be their year, and 1980/81 was no exception for Darlington.

The Quakers had been busy during the summer. The previous season had finished with yet another application for re-election.

Again, they had been safely voted in, along with Hereford United, Crewe Alexandra and Rochdale, the latter surviving by the skin of their teeth after beating Altrincham by only one vote.

Manager Billy Elliott reacted to this by releasing 11 players and vowing that, from now on, Darlington would rely on a much smaller, younger playing staff. Clive Nattress, Jimmy Cochrane, Derek Craig, Dave

Crosson, Ron Ferguson, Phil Owers, John Peachey, Phil Taylor, Peter Bainbridge, Bryan Kent and Keith Coleman were all let go. Elliott also scrapped the reserve team and replaced it with a new youth team under the stewardship of former Sunderland defender Ritchie Pitt. The team, which included Fred Barber and Brian Honour, who later would star in the first team, would compete in the Northern Intermediate League.

Only four new signings were made before the season kicked off. Goalkeeper Pat Cuff was signed from Millwall, defenders Alan Kamara and Peter Skipper came from York City and Hull City respectively, and midfielder David Speedie from Barnsley. All four of them made their league debuts in the opening-day fixture against Northampton.

By this time I was 15 and could communicate much better, so my mother decided to take me to the games, leave me there, do her shopping, and then come back for me, something she did on this particular day. Only Cuff and Harry Charlton were over the age of 24 in a very young and inexperienced side, which was captained by Donald Ball who, at 18, was the youngest skipper in the Football League.

In the Feethams sunshine, Darlington won 1-0 with a John Stalker goal just before half-time, in front of 1,763 fans.

It was the start of what was to be a much better season for the Quakers.

DARLINGTON V WIGAN ATHLETIC – 1980/81

The team made an average start to the 1980/81 season with two wins and a draw from their first five games, so that when Wigan Athletic visited Feethams on 13 September the Quakers sat in mid-table with five points. The Latics were making their third visit to Feethams since replacing Southport as a Football League side in 1978. Their previous two visits had both resulted in draws.

The build-up to the game was dominated by transfer news, Elliott finally managing to land one of his long-term targets when he secured the services of left-back Harry Wilson from Preston North End. The 26-year-old had 180 league appearances under his belt in spells at Burnley, Brighton and Hove Albion, and Preston and would add some much-needed experience to help the youngsters in the team. Wilson would slot straight into the team in his preferred position to replace Dave McLean, who could then move into his preferred position in midfield, instead of Ian Hamilton, who had been ruled out with flu. Pat Cuff failed a late fitness test, so former Nottingham Forest youngster Kevin Barry continued his recent spell in goal. The visitors had themselves strengthened their side by signing defender Brian Kettle from Liverpool for £30,000. Kettle would make his debut in this game.

A crowd of 2,020 were at Feethams to see this match (I was among them). We witnessed the visitors have an early spell of sustained pressure which kept the home defence busy, but they were unable to trouble keeper Barry, Dave McMullen going closest when he headed wide. Darlington, however, weathered the early storm and took the lead in the 14th minute. New signing Wilson played a perfect through ball to John Stalker who shrugged off a weak tackle by Neil Davids before shooting calmly across goalkeeper John Brown into the far corner of the net. The lead only lasted for ten minutes before the visitors drew level with a gift equaliser when McLean tried to steer a right-wing David Fretwell cross out for a corner but only succeeded in turning the ball inside his own post. Harry Charlton and Alan Walsh both went close as the home side pressed forward, but with Tommy Gore working well in midfield, the visitors were always a threat. Darlington finished the half well on top with three corners in quick succession but couldn't make the pressure tell.

The visitors started the second half strongly with substitute David Glenn hitting the angle of post and bar before McMullen missed the target from 12 yards when in the clear. Darlington hit back and regained the lead in the 77th minute. Speedie played a brilliant through ball into the path of Stalker, who again outstripped Davids before lobbing over the advancing Brown from an acute angle. Athletic recovered and Frank Corrigan squandered a great chance to equalise when he headed Gore's cross wide from only five yards out.

Stalker sealed the victory in injury time when he completed his hat-trick with a fine solo goal. He turned Davids and Colin Methven on the edge of the visitors' box and fired towards goal. His shot was beaten out by Brown but Stalker snapped up the rebound to celebrate the first Feethams hat-trick since Eddie Rowles had put three goals past Scarborough in the FA Cup in 1976. While Stalker stole all the headlines with his goals, Alan Kamara was man of the match with an outstanding performance at right-back. New boy Wilson also had an impressive debut but unsurprisingly faded in the last 20 minutes due to a lack of match fitness. I can remember being over the moon as my mother pushed me home from the ground.

The 3-1 win took the Quakers up to ninth in the table, only three points behind leaders Lincoln, and hopes were high that they could mount a concerted push for promotion. In typical Darlington fashion though, they shot themselves in the foot by losing their next four games.

DARLINGTON V MANSFIELD TOWN – 1980/81

I was lucky enough to be at Feethams in February 1981, when Darlington played against Mansfield Town for the first game to be played on a Sunday under the Football League's initiative to allow clubs to trial moving matches to Sundays.

With national television and press coverage focused on the game, our average gate of 2,500 had swelled to an impressive 5,932. According to local reporter Mike Amos in the *Northern Echo*, the club had arranged for 2,000 programmes to be printed and had purchased a thousand pies, all of which were sold!

After Ian Hamilton converted a penalty, Mansfield scored twice and we needed a rare headed goal in the 88th minute from regular goalscorer Alan Walsh to earn us a creditable 2-2 draw.

Following the game, I was left wondering why we couldn't attract such big crowds every week. It was certainly strange that the club more than doubled their gate for a Sunday match. I certainly found it hard to comprehend as these thoughts went through my head during my journey home.

As a footnote to 1980/81, Darlo spent the whole season just out of reach of the promotion race, comfortably in the top half. The much-improved season was due in no small part to the potent strike force of John Stalker and Alan Walsh, who managed 40 goals between them throughout the nine months. Walsh finished with 23 goals and Stalker with 17.

The Quakers eventually finished in eighth place, with 49 points, in the days of two points for a win. This was the highest I'd seen them finish in the eight years that I'd supported them. Attendances hovered around the 2,000 mark for much of the season, but ended with an average of 2,537, due mainly to 7,155 seeing the derby with Hartlepool, and several better crowds due to the experiment with Sunday football. Darlington were actually the first club in the country to try this, and had to have it specially sanctioned at a Football League meeting.

It was in an attempt to avoid fixture clashes with Middlesbrough, Sunderland and Newcastle and so improve attendances. It seemed to work as well. So, Darlington Football Club were pioneers in introducing Sunday football to the nation, long before Sky had even been thought of!

Adult admission to Feethams was £1.20 in the 1980/81 season although, at that time charging admission wasn't allowed on a Sunday, so the club charged £1.20 for a team sheet, which automatically gained you entry into the ground.

DARLINGTON V SCUNTHORPE UNITED – 1981/82

Another season, another financial crisis at Darlington Football Club. This particular one was 1981/82, and although the Quakers had experienced many financial problems during their 99-year history, this one was so severe that it threatened the very existence of the football club. At the AGM in November, record losses of £48,000 were reported from the previous season, bringing the total debt to £74,000. It was also reported that the club was losing over £800 per week, but chairman Leslie Moore insisted that there was no cash crisis.

However, things became considerably worse in December and January when three consecutive home games were postponed due to bad weather, which meant that no money was coming in through the turnstiles. The problem reached crisis point at the end of January when a special press conference was called at Feethams and Moore announced that if £50,000 wasn't raised within the next six weeks, the club would fold. They were now £95,000 in debt and had no cash available to pay any of their bills, with a weekly wage bill of £4,000.

There was a very real danger that Darlington would not survive to celebrate their centenary year the following season. The record losses from the previous season were even more worrying because they coincided with the team having one of their best seasons for many years, together with a very small squad. Manager Billy Elliott continued this ploy and basically relied on 15 players throughout the 1981/82 season. His only significant signing during the summer had been Kenny Mitchell, brought in from Newcastle United.

When Scunthorpe United visited Feethams on Wednesday, 17 February, they found their hosts struggling to find any kind of form. They were in a run of only one win from seven games since the turn of the year. Happily for Quakers fans, the one win that they had managed had been 2-1 at Hartlepool United.

They had prepared for the Scunthorpe game with a 3-1 reverse at Peterborough United, where all three Posh goals were down to defensive mistakes. Elliott threatened changes, but found his options limited due to the size of his squad, and ended up naming an unchanged team for the visit of the Humberside-based side. Darlington sat in 17th place in the Fourth Division table with 25 points from 26 games. Their visitors sat two places lower, in 19th, level on points but with a game in hand, so the game was important to both clubs in their battle to avoid the bottom four re-election places. I have to say, I wasn't optimistic as I took my place in the East Stand paddock. It was half-term so luckily I could attend this match.

The appeal for extra support seemed to fall on deaf ears as only 1,633 braved the cold and rain. They saw the home side make a shaky start as United snatched the lead as early as the fourth minute. A weak defensive header by Kevan Smith was seized upon by David Stewart who blasted home from 20 yards out. Darlington played their way back into the game and equalised in the 22nd minute when Smith made amends for his error by creating the opening. He headed down Dave McLean's free kick and David Speedie hooked in his eighth goal of the season. Play was scrappy until after the break with both sides failing to carve out any clear-cut chances, although Darlo were always uncomfortable against the quick Scunthorpe counter-attacks.

Two goals in two minutes in the second half turned the game dramatically. The home side were awarded a penalty after 61 minutes when Andy Keeley needlessly handled the ball just inside the box. McLean sent the keeper, Paul Johnson, the wrong way from the spot but the keeper managed to save with his feet, and then recovered brilliantly to parry Speedie's follow-up. In the goalmouth scramble that followed, McLean managed to hook the ball home at the third attempt. Two minutes later it was 3-1, as a trademark drive by Alan Walsh from the edge of the area was palmed away by Johnson but only as far as Peter Skipper, who tapped the loose ball into the empty net for his first goal of the season.

The Quakers were now in complete control and it was no surprise when they scored their fourth in the 70th minute. Again it was from the penalty spot, again for a handball, this time awarded against Tony Arins. Walsh took on the responsibility on this occasion and made no mistake by hammering home an unstoppable shot. The margin of victory could have been even greater as there was still time for John Stalker to slice an easy chance wide of the post, and Scunthorpe were left a well-beaten side. As I watched the game, I can remember how lucky we were to have a player like Alan Walsh in our team. His running with the ball was the difference between the two teams, in what was a deserved Darlington victory.

ROCHDALE V DARLINGTON – 1981/82

A month after the Scunthorpe match, I travelled to Rochdale on the supporters' club coach. Rather than me miss the game, the supporters' club provided me with a helper, as for various reasons none of my friends could attend the game.

The Quakers twice threw away the lead that day. Rochdale grabbed their winner in the last few minutes when Kevan Smith played a woefully short backpass to his keeper, Pat Cuff, which Mark Hilditch intercepted, rolling the ball into the unguarded net.

The final score was 3-2, with David Speedie getting both our goals, but it was what happened off the pitch that sticks in my mind rather than the game itself.

Since we arrived in Rochdale well before the kick-off, my helper and I went for a drink in their social club behind the Main Stand.

We had only been there a few minutes when a full-scale riot broke out after a dozen or so Darlington hooligans entered the bar. During the course of the riot, a fearsomely tattooed skinhead came up to me and asked, very politely, 'Do you mind if I take this table?' – with mine being the only one left intact at that point in time. Not wishing to see my glass of lager lying smashed at my feet, I replied, 'Let me pick up my drink first,' and so he said, 'No problem, Paul.' Although he seemingly knew me by name, I didn't know him from Adam. He then proceeded to lift up the table and clobbered some poor unfortunate Rochdale supporter over the head with it!

I can remember seeing the same skinhead later, lying flat on his back with his mouth wide open, drinking beer from the tap on the bar. The barmaid tried to prevent him with cries of, 'No, no, stop it!' but she was just crudely told to 'f*** off!'

Another lout became honorary barman and proclaimed, 'Drinks are on the house, today!' while others simply clambered over the bar and helped themselves. As for me, I sat there with my half of lager in the midst of all that mayhem. It was like being in the eye of a storm.

The next thing I saw was a well-aimed kick from a Doc Martens boot smashing the trophy cabinet. The looters then paraded the cups and shields as if they had just been presented with them after a Wembley cup final victory.

Later, some of the other louts held a competition to see who could excrete in the pockets of the snooker table – a case of who could pot the brown first, you might say! One moron actually rubbed his backside on the cloth and left behind a dirty skidmark while another lad nicked the snooker balls, probably to use them later as missiles – you could see them bulging in his trouser pockets as he left. In short, they absolutely wrecked the place.

The police didn't show up for at least half an hour, by which time the culprits had vanished, and because there were no video cameras installed on the premises in those days no prosecutions were ever brought. After the hooligans had left, the barmaid said, 'I've never seen such dirty bastards before in all my life,' and she was certainly right on that score.

I have to say, the scenes I witnessed that day will be etched in my memory forever.

One final comment about my helper; while everything was going on, he sat there rigid in his seat, unable to move. After he dropped me off at home, I never saw him again at any Darlington games. He must have been too traumatised to go back.

Anyway, back to the football. Following the Rochdale defeat, Darlo went on to finish the season really strongly. They climbed as high as tenth in the table at one point, eventually finishing their campaign in 13th, with 58 points from their 46 games. Top scorers in the league were David Speedie with 17 and Alan Walsh with 13.

Regarding the fundraising, the whole town rallied round with various events and money-making schemes (I went knocking on people's doors in my area and raised a sizeable sum – I can't remember exactly how much) to raise money towards the amount required to get the club through to the end of the season. Two attractive friendly games were also organised to boost the survival fund. Alan Durban's Sunderland visited Feethams at the beginning of March and Lawrie McMenemy brought his star-studded Southampton side to visit in April.

This ensured that the £50,000 target was reached before the end of the season. Interestingly, Darlington won the Southampton match 5-2 with Speedie helping himself to a hat-trick. Alan Walsh and Tony McFadden netted the other two goals.

DARLINGTON V ROCHDALE – 1982/83

As mentioned earlier, serious financial problems had blighted the 1981/82 season. But manager Billy Elliott had still led the team to a creditable mid-table position. The fans had raised £50,000 to ensure that the club completed the season and the coffers were further boosted in the summer as Peter Skipper left for Hull City in a £10,000 tribunal transfer and David Speedie was sold to Chelsea for £65,000. Elliott wasn't given any of the money to replace two of his most influential players and for the second year in a row, the club kicked off the 1982/83 season with a threadbare squad of only 15 professionals. He would have to supplement his squad with loan signings and former youth team players as and when required. The youth team had been disbanded and a reserve team had been entered in the newly formed Northern League Division Two.

Many of the previous season's youth team were still with the club and made up the bulk of the reserve team. Injuries to John Stalker and Gavin Liddle meant that the team virtually picked itself for the opening-day fixture at home to Rochdale in front of a disappointing crowd of 1,672.

The match took place on the same day as Kevin Keegan made his Newcastle United debut at St James' Park. Darlington's home games coincided with Newcastle's all season, so their attendances suffered accordingly because of this.

Former Sunderland midfielder Tim Gilbert (now sadly no longer with us) was signed from Cardiff City, forward Barry Dunn (also a former Sunderland man) signed following his release by Preston and full-back Trevor Brissett (also sadly deceased) joined from Port Vale. Midfielder Billy Ingham signed from Bradford City, but then within days shocked Elliott by announcing that he was retiring from the game. Not the ideal start to a new season.

Brissett, Gilbert and Dunn all made their debuts against the Dale, who were managed by former Quaker Peter Madden. The Lancashire side had finished the previous season fourth from bottom of the table and arrived at Feethams with eight new signings in their squad.

Darlo fans saw the game kick off in bright sunshine and it was the visitors who threatened first. Left-winger Peter Farrell curled a 20-yard shot narrowly over Pat Cuff's bar in the fourth minute. Darlington hit back and should have taken the lead in the tenth minute. Alan Walsh and Tony McFadden combined well to create an opening for Roger Wicks but he mishit his shot from eight yards out and Dale keeper Chris Pearce managed to scramble the ball around the post.

The home side were beginning to take control of the game with Tim Gilbert spraying passes around the midfield with his classy left foot and his fellow debutant Barry Dunn showing superb dribbling skills down the left wing. Watching from my usual vantage point, I couldn't help but be impressed by his dazzling performance. Dunn's signing had allowed Walsh to move into a more central striking role and he was causing new Dale centre-half Jack Trainer all manner of problems, and it was no surprise when he opened the scoring after 17 minutes. Rochdale failed to clear a Dave McLean corner, the ball dropped to Walsh 12 yards out and his instinctive first-time shot flew past Pearce just inside the post.

The Quakers were well on top now and increased their lead on the half hour. It followed a fine, flowing move down the left wing that involved Harry Wilson, Dunn and McFadden, the ball eventually being squared to Walsh, who crashed an unstoppable shot home from 20 yards out. Pearce got his right hand to it but couldn't stop it on its way into the roof of the net.

The second half began with the visitors in much more determined mood, and they gained control of the midfield areas and started to get on top. Darlington always looked threatening on the break though with Dunn, Walsh and McFadden linking impressively. Dunn hit one long-range effort that Pearce did well to save at the foot of his post, and shortly afterwards Walsh had a shot deflected for a corner. In their best spell, Dale went close to pulling a goal back, first with a Barry Wellings header that was deflected goalwards by Kevan Smith but was brilliantly saved by Pat Cuff, who showed great agility in changing direction to keep the ball out. Then Wellings curled a fine shot just wide.

Darlington went looking for a third goal when Walsh crossed towards McFadden but he missed the easiest chance of the game when he blazed over from only six yards out. Shortly after that, Wicks put another chance wide when it looked easier to score. Just when it looked as if Rochdale might force themselves back into the game, Darlo hit them with a classic counter-attack in the 80th minute. McFadden led a quick break down the left and played a perfect through ball to Dunn who fired home with a first-time shot on the run in front of the Tin Shed. This gave the home side a deserved opening-day victory.

CREWE ALEXANDRA V DARLINGTON – 1982/83

The second game of the 1982/83 season was the following Friday night, 3 September, away to Crewe Alexandra. Manager Billy Elliott had no hesitation in naming an unchanged side. His only selection dilemma was who to pick as substitute. John Stalker and Gavin Liddle were now available, as was teenager Brian Honour who had impressed for the reserves in midweek, but the number 12 shirt went to Dave Hawker, who had been re-signed on a short-term contract following his release the previous season.

Crewe had finished the previous season bottom of the Fourth Division, an incredible 15 points adrift of the next club above them. They had managed only six wins all season and were determined to do better this time around. They were managed by Arfon Griffiths and had extensively reshaped their squad over the summer. They included eight new faces in their side and had opened the season with a narrow 1-0 defeat at Chester.

A crowd of 1,739 were at Gresty Road for the match. I travelled to the match on the supporters' club coach with my friend John Gray. We saw Darlington turn in a complete performance and dominate the game from start to finish. They took the lead in the 19th minute when a fierce Alan Walsh drive was blocked by home goalkeeper Steve Smith. The ball rebounded to the edge of the box where it was met by Tim Gilbert who drove the ball home.

The Quakers continued to drive forward and had two strong claims for penalties turned down. Barry Dunn was brought down by home defender Neil Salathiel when in full flight, shortly after a Dunn shot appeared to be fisted away by central defender Bob Scott. Crewe were hanging on but conceded a second goal five minutes before half-time. Harry Wilson played the ball to the edge of the Crewe area to Tony McFadden who superbly nodded it back into the path of Dave McLean. His fierce drive from 20 yards out flew into the roof of the net. The half ended with an injury concern for the impressive Gilbert who went down after a clash of heads with Bernard Purdie.

The shaken and concussed Gilbert was unable to continue and was replaced at half-time by Hawker. The change didn't seem to disrupt the visitors much. They still played all the flowing football and threatened more goals every time they attacked. Their third goal came after 56 minutes when Alan Walsh cracked a shot against the foot of the post and Dunn coolly picked his spot and swept the rebound home.

In a rare home attack, Crewe gave themselves some hope with a goal of their own on 62 minutes. A Clive Evans shot came back off the woodwork and Steve Craven reacted quicker than Kevan Smith to stab the ball home. The home team's revival never really happened though and Darlington increased their lead in the 70th minute. A McLean corner was flicked on by Walsh and volleyed home by Smith at the far post. The waves of attacks by the visitors continued and they scored their fifth of the night in the 86th minute. A sweeping 60-yard pass from Walsh sent McFadden racing into the box. He held off Scott's challenge and drilled his shot between keeper Smith and the near post. There was still time for Crewe to grab a second consolation goal on 88 minutes, when Evans headed home a Dave Goodwin cross after a defensive mix-up.

John and I were certainly happy as we headed home on the coach.

ALDERSHOT V DARLINGTON – 1982/83

A run of only two wins in 23 games saw Darlington tumble down the whole of the Fourth Division table to occupy bottom place by the beginning of February 1983. In an attempt to stop the rot, manager Billy Elliott signed two players on loan from Newcastle United – Kevin Todd to play up front, and David Barton to fill the problem position of centre-half.

The introduction of these two players certainly had the desired effect and two wins in February lifted Darlington off the bottom of the table. By the time their visit to Aldershot came around on Tuesday, 1 March, Darlington sat second from bottom with 29 points from their 30 games. Aldershot sat comfortably in mid-table with 39 points from 31 games, with one defeat in their previous eight games; they were in a decent run of form and would provide a stiff test. They were managed by ex-Quakers coach and manager Len Walker.

Elliott named an unchanged 11 for the long trip. They'd suffered a 3-1 home defeat in their previous game to promotion-chasing Colchester United, but the manager had been happy with the performance and had blamed missed chances for the defeat. He admitted that his team had to be much more accurate with their shooting in order to get the results that their play deserved. 'Prophetic words,' I thought. Unfortunately, I couldn't attend the game, as I was let down with a lift at the last minute – but here's what Simon Weatherill wrote about this incredible match:

'A crowd of 1,400 were at the Recreation Ground to see the home side make a bright start to the game. They suffered a setback as early as the eighth minute though, when centre-half Alan Wooler limped off with a groin strain. He was replaced by midfielder Colin Fielder. Aldershot took time to reorganise their defence and the Quakers took full advantage and snatched the lead in the 12th minute. Dave McLean played an inch-perfect pass through the home defence and Alan Walsh blasted the ball home with the Shots defenders appealing for offside.

'The visitors took total control and should have added to their lead. They forced three corners in as many minutes and Kevin Todd wasted some good opportunities as the home defence found his pace almost impossible to deal with. Aldershot's task got even harder in the 35th minute when left-back Ian Gillard was stretchered off with a back injury after an aerial collision with Todd, meaning they had to play out the remaining 55 minutes with ten men.

'Any hopes Aldershot had of getting back into the game were quashed with two more Darlo goals at the start of the second half. On 46 minutes a Tim Gilbert corner resulted in a goalmouth scramble with the ball forced home by Todd. Two minutes later, another Gilbert corner was headed home by Dave Barton. In a rare attack, Aldershot managed to pull a goal back in the 52nd minute when Stuart Robinson broke clear and ran through a static defence to hammer a great shot past the helpless Pat Cuff in the Darlington goal. The ten men were starting to struggle though and in the 69th minute Tony McFadden capitalised on a defensive mistake by Dale Banton and fired home the fourth goal. Todd grabbed his second, and Darlington's fifth, with a fierce drive from the edge of the box in the 81st minute, and then two minutes later he completed his hat-trick when he fired home from close range.'

When I heard the score on the radio, I was gutted that I hadn't been able to make it to the game. Being let down made it even more frustrating. It was a lesson learned and I never made arrangements with that person again as he had decided to go out drinking the night before our supposed trip and wasn't fit enough to drive the following day. As the reader can imagine, I wasn't impressed.

The 6-1 victory was Darlington's biggest away win since beating Durham City 7-3 in a Third Division North game in 1921, and it lifted the Quakers four places in the table and took them clear of the dreaded re-election zone.

DARLINGTON V MANSFIELD TOWN – 1982/83

This game sticks in my mind for a couple of reasons, one of which was the fact that as my mother pushed my through the town centre to the ground, it was packed with protestors who were there to vent their anger at British Railway's proposed closure of the Shildon wagon works, which provided a lot of employment for people who lived in the Darlington area. Unfortunately, the demonstrators were fighting a lost cause as British Rail shut the company down a year later.

Up until the 1-0 victory against Tranmere in February 1983, a month prior to this match, Darlo had not registered a win of any description since the previous November and, with this in mind, the home attendances were declining. Already we had gates hovering just above the 1,000 mark and it came as no surprise to me that I witnessed the lowest ever league crowd at Feethams on that day of only 952 paying customers. This was the second reason why this match sticks in my mind to this day.

Prior to the game, David Barton failed a fitness test and was replaced by youngster Jeff Wilson. To compound matters, experienced left-back Harry Wilson limped off after a heavy challenge during the first half and was replaced by 17-year-old substitute David Wakefield, who was an England youth international, with one solitary cap to his name.

In what was a lacklustre display, the Stags had two players sent off, namely John Matthews in the 49th minute and Gary Mickleson in the 74th.

Despite the fact that Mansfield only had nine men, the home side could hardly muster a shot to trouble the visiting goalkeeper, Rod Arnold, in what can only be described as a shocking performance.

At the final whistle of this goalless draw, the players were booed off the pitch and there was an angry demonstration at the rear of the East Stand from a couple of hundred of the Darlington fans who had bothered to attend the match.

Like them, I wasn't impressed and didn't mutter a word to my mother during our journey home.

DARLINGTON V STOCKPORT COUNTY –
1982/83

The recent run of good results prior didn't seem to inspire the supporters too much and only 1,012 turned out for the Stockport game. This was slightly better than the attendance against Mansfield, but still very poor. The crowd, which included me, witnessed a stuttering start by the home side, who, despite their recent improvement in form, had still only won one home game in the previous four months. Their nervousness showed as the visitors enjoyed the best of the opening half.

County took the lead in the 38th minute with a straightforward corner routine. Dean Emerson's flag kick was met by Tommy Sword who scored with an unstoppable header. They could have increased their lead before but goalkeeper Fred Barber, who was making his league debut following an injury to regular number one Pat Cuff, produced two brilliant saves to keep out Nigel Smith and Mike Power. Stockport went into the break with a comfortable 1-0 lead, with the Quakers seemingly sliding towards yet another home defeat.

Barber continued his man-of-the-match performance by saving twice more from Power at the start of the second half, before providing an assist for Alan Walsh's equaliser in the 65th minute. He launched a hefty kick deep into Stockport territory that found Walsh breaking through a gap in the centre of County's defence. He rounded visiting keeper Brian Lloyd and slotted into the net from an acute angle.

Peter Cartwright, signed on loan from Newcastle United prior to the match, was not to be outdone by his fellow debutant, and then took centre stage by creating the opening for Darlo's second goal, in the 75th minute. He ploughed through three tackles in a determined run in central midfield and played the ball out wide to Walsh, who made progress down the left and crossed to the far post, where the ball was met by the onrushing Dave McLean who headed home. The victory was completed in the last minute when Tony McFadden outpaced three defenders before drawing Lloyd and sliding the ball wide of the advancing keeper. Three goals in the last 25 minutes had turned what looked like being Darlington's eighth home defeat of the season into an important victory that moved them up another two places in the table.

Man of the match Barber continued his great form and kept his place in goal for the remainder of the season. He became regular first choice and went on to make 163 appearances for the club over the next three years before being transferred to Everton for £50,000 in March 1986. I had seen him develop for three years in both the reserve and youth teams, so it came as no surprise to me when he grabbed his first-team opportunity with both hands, so to speak.

Barber was one of six of the previous year's youth team who had progressed through into the first team during the 1982/83 season. Brian Honour, David Young, David Wakefield, Gavin Liddle and Jeff Wilson also turned out in Fourth Division matches, something Darlington were really proud of at the time.

STOCKPORT COUNTY V DARLINGTON – 1983/84

Season 1983/84 saw Darlington appoint a new manager in Cyril Knowles, the former England international and Tottenham Hotspur full-back replacing the hard-working and indeed likeable Billy Elliott.

I first met my long-term friend Stephen Lowson at a home match in September 1983. We got on really well together and ended up going to see the team play away at Stockport County in October of that year, which I'll recount below.

The pair of us caught the train at Darlington railway station where Stephen bought a copy of the *Northern Echo* to read on our journey. As he was engrossed in the sports section on the back page, I was in turn highly amused by the front-page headline which related to Cecil Parkinson, the then secretary of state for trade and industry, who had resigned from his post the previous day. His hand had been forced as fresh details were revealed about his extramarital affair with his former secretary, Sara Keays. I remember thinking to myself how quickly people can fall from grace. Before this scandal was made public, Mr Parkinson was Margaret Thatcher's darling and could do no wrong in her eyes. How mistaken she had been about him.

Anyway, after I'd finished reading about the extramarital exploits of the unfortunate former cabinet minister, Stephen brought me back down to earth by telling me that, according to the newspaper, Darlington were in the midst of an injury crisis with seven players on the treatment table. In fact, Knowles had asked the Football League to postpone the game and was incensed after they turned down his request.

During our journey, Stephen produced quite a sizeable lunchbox containing several strawberry-jam sandwiches, which his mother had made for him, together with a carton of yoghurt and a spoon. When he had polished off his bait, I asked him what he was going to do with the empty box, to which he mischievously replied, 'Watch me!' He then opened the train window and threw it out, along with the empty carton and spoon. I just shook my head in disbelief at his antics. I found the whole episode highly amusing.

Following our arrival at Manchester Piccadilly station, we immediately boarded the service to Stockport, as it was already on the opposite platform waiting to depart.

After visiting several pubs in the town centre, we headed for Edgeley Park, rather the worse for wear, it has to be said.

Once inside the ground, Stephen carried me up the steps so that we could sit together in the seats. Over the tannoy we learned that Bobby Hulse, who was signed the previous week from French side Stade Quimpérois on a free transfer, was in the team as a replacement for the experienced John Craggs who was relegated to the bench.

Also, teenager David Wakefield played what was only his second full league game for the club.

Darlington were outplayed in the first half and were fortunate that goalkeeper Fred Barber was at his best, making several excellent saves. However, the Stockport pressure continued unabated in the second period when they eventually took the lead through Mick Quinn, who later signed for Newcastle United.

The game was sewn up when, in the 87th minute, north-east lad Oshor Williams picked up the ball on the halfway line, dribbling past several Darlington players on the way, before beating Barber with a well-struck shot. This was Darlington's fourth defeat in their five away games of the new season.

With the applause of the home fans still ringing in our ears, we made our way somewhat disconsolately towards the railway station to commence our journey home.

BRISTOL CITY V DARLINGTON – 1983/84

In March 1984, I couldn't go with Stephen to the game at Bristol City as I already had a long-standing agreement to go there with my old friend Barry Wetherill.

As Barry got me on board the Intercity 125 train early on Saturday morning at Darlington's Bank Top station, we soon realised that we would be sitting in the same coach as the players.

Having lifted me into a vacant seat, Barry stowed my folded wheelchair in the luggage area near the coach door, and I found myself sitting opposite the club captain, Dave McLean.

When he suggested a game of cards, our striker John Hannah came to make a foursome with Barry and me.

To my surprise, we ended up playing my favourite game, Three Card Brag, and I ended up winning handsomely. In our final game, the stake crept up inexorably from 50p to £1, to £5 and then to £10 until I mischievously increased it to £50.

By this time the pot contained well over £200 and John Hannah would have needed £50 just to see me, so he threw in his strong hand of three queens. My bluff had worked. When he saw me scooping up the pot with my miserable hand of ten high, he quite understandably exclaimed, 'You bastard!'

Hannah had joined us in October 1983 as a non-contract player, serving us well as a burly no-nonsense centre-forward. In many ways his aggressive style of play reminded me of Ron Ferguson. Anyway, I felt guilty about taking so much money from him, especially as he was still on strike (he was a miner at the time), so I gave him £50 back and he thanked me for being a 'gentleman'.

When we arrived at Bristol Temple Meads station, the players had a coach booked to take them to the ground. Cyril Knowles offered to give us a lift but rather than have the hassle of carrying me up a flight of steps, we thanked him for his kind offer, politely declined and caught a taxi instead.

The match turned out to be a great disappointment, with the home side well on top – the Robins forced 13 corners to Darlo's one. Frustratingly, in the 84th minute, we were denied a point when Keith Curle's cross dropped to the right foot of Trevor Morgan, who made no mistake. John Hannah, on the other hand, missed a sitter late on in the game when he completely miscued his shot. After what had happened earlier with me and the game of cards, I suppose it just wasn't going to be his day.

Although we came back on the same train as the players, they were naturally dejected after their defeat so we left them to their own devices.

The improvement in our league position only ended up being slight, and we eventually finished 14th. Altogether, I went to 13 away games that season, mostly with Stephen.

TORQUAY UNITED V DARLINGTON – 1984/85

The 1984/85 season turned out to be one of the better campaigns in the history of Darlington Football Club, although bad news on the transfer front in the summer threatened to derail the manager's plans before it had even started. Star striker Alan Walsh left and signed for Bristol City for a paltry £18,000, a fee set by the transfer tribunal. Cyril Knowles, now in his second season, wasted no time in signing his replacement, paying Barnsley £6,000 for Carl Airey, a signing that was to prove inspired over the coming months. Knowles also added winger Mark Miller from Doncaster Rovers and midfielder Mitch Cook from Scarborough.

The new signings still meant that the Quakers kicked off the new season with a threadbare squad and injuries to Cook and Mike Angus meant that in the early weeks Knowles often only had 11 or 12 fit players to choose from. Despite the shortage of numbers, his side made a solid start to the season with two wins and four draws from the first six games, seeing Darlo sitting comfortably in sixth place in the Fourth Division table with ten points.

Knowles was always looking to bolster his squad and signed two extra midfielders. Graeme Aldred (now sadly no longer with us) joined after being released by Newcastle, and Steve Tupling came in, initially on a month's loan, from Carlisle United. He also brought in the vastly experienced Scottish international Willie Young as defensive cover. The 32-year-old centre-half had played nearly 300 top-flight games for Tottenham Hotspur, Arsenal and Nottingham Forest and had played alongside Knowles in Spurs' defence in the 1970s.

Only four Darlington fans in a Ford Capri made the 350-mile journey to Torquay United in September 1984, and I am proud to say I was one of them. To make matters worse, the match was an evening kick-off, so we set off at about ten in the morning. I travelled with a lad called Gavin and two other supporters, whose names escape me with the passing of time.

Stopping twice at service stations en route, we arrived in Torquay at about five o'clock and after some fish and chips to line our stomachs we also had a few pints in a pub near the ground.

Prior to the kick-off, it quickly became apparent that Steve Tupling and Willie Young were making their debuts for the Quakers.

Although we forced 14 corners to the home side's five during the course of the game, that was a misleading statistic since the Gulls hit the post twice and scored in the tenth minute. By contrast, Darlo played abysmally and were lucky to be only 1-0 down at the break. The Gulls were so much the better side that I do believe if it had been a boxing match the referee would have intervened and stopped it. But we hung on gamely and got a corner with three minutes to go, which was taken by Dave McLean. The ball was flicked on at the near post by Colin Ross and Carl Airey gleefully headed in the equaliser.

All I can remember is going absolutely mental, celebrating the goal, as the Torquay supporters were predictably singing, 'You're going to get your f****ng heads kicked in!' I think they must have been quite upset, because two policemen had to escort the four of us back to our car for our own safety.

On our way home, we bumped into Cyril Knowles at a service station as the team coach had stopped there as well. When he saw how cramped the conditions were in the car, he said, 'My God, you lot look squashed in there! Do you want me to take Paul with us?' I gladly accepted his offer, and Kevan Smith carried me on board the team coach.

This was the first time that I'd met Cyril to talk to, although I did see him during the aforementioned trip to Bristol City the season prior, and from then on we became firm friends. I sat with him at the front of the coach and we chatted for the rest of the journey. He admitted that we'd been very lucky that night, but as he said, 'It's the sign of a good side that can play below par and still come away with a draw.' He certainly struck me as being very tactically astute as we chatted away into the early hours of the morning.

When we eventually arrived in Darlington, Gavin was waiting for me outside Feethams and the driver of the Ford Capri gave us both a lift back home.

ALDERSHOT V DARLINGTON – 1984/85

All three of our new signings were in the team for the long trip to Aldershot, a game that I went to on the supporters' club coach with Stephen Lowson. This was Darlington's seventh game of the season and once again they were struggling to find 11 fit players. Regular central defensive partners Kevan Smith and Phil Lloyd were both missing after they were injured in the previous week's victory over Scunthorpe United, Smith with a dislocated shoulder and Lloyd with ankle ligament damage.

Willie Young would make his second appearance for the club alongside Peter Johnson, who moved across from his more familiar left-back position to play in the centre. Dave McLean would drop back from midfield to play at left-back. The only regular member of the defence playing in his correct position would be John Craggs at right-back, although he had to pass a fitness test on a troublesome ankle before being cleared to play. Mitch Cook made his long-awaited debut on the left of midfield. He'd missed the start of the season after injuring his knee in a pre-season friendly and although not fully fit he was pressed into service due to the sheer shortage of numbers.

Finances dictated that the Quakers travelled down south by coach on the day of the game. Heavy traffic meant that the team only arrived at the Recreation Ground 90 minutes before kick-off. Hardly ideal preparation, but the side made light of the hardship by taking the lead in the first minute. Cook made an instant impact with a superb through ball into the path of Kevin Todd (by now with the club on a permanent basis), who lashed a fierce shot past home keeper David Coles to give the visitors the early lead and stun the home crowd of 2,045.

Aldershot stormed back and put the makeshift Darlington defence under real pressure but squandered several chances when a bit of composure in front of goal would have seen them level. During this period of pressure, the visitors looked dangerous on the break with the pace of Kevin Todd and Carl Airey always a threat. Darlo suffered a blow in the 25th minute when Colin Ross had to leave the field with a recurrence of an old knee injury. He was replaced by John Hannah who went up front with Todd dropping into a deeper position.

The Shots eventually equalised in the 37th minute with a close-range effort by Martin Foyle, a £20,000 summer signing from Southampton. This effort was already Foyle's fifth goal of the season. Hannah had an immediate chance to restore the visitors' lead but his header from a Todd cross was just over. However, he made no mistake two minutes later when he picked up a Steve Tupling through ball on the edge of the box and hammered it on the turn past the helpless keeper to give Darlington a 2-1 half-time lead.

An assured second-half performance, with Young looking particularly dominant at the back, should have been enough for the visitors to comfortably take the points, but in typical Darlington fashion they managed to make life difficult for themselves. They increased their lead in the 76th minute with another Hannah goal. Airey's shot was blocked but Hannah found himself unmarked in front of goal to walk the rebound into an empty net. The two-goal cushion lasted only two minutes, however, as Fred Barber gifted the Shots a second. His poor clearance went straight to Dale Banton who swept it straight back into the net to make it 3-2.

Barber then redeemed himself with two outstanding saves as the home side looked for an equaliser, but Hannah made the points safe in the 91st minute when he headed home Cook's cross to complete his hat-trick. There was still time for Aldershot to hit back as a scramble in the visitors' goalmouth allowed Banton to fire home his second with the last kick of the match. Stephen and I were overjoyed at the final whistle, and our journey home somehow didn't feel as long as the seemingly never-ending one that had started at six in the morning.

The 4-3 victory moved the Quakers up to fifth in the table and maintained their unbeaten start to the season. Unfortunately, that Aldershot match proved to be Colin Ross's last as a professional footballer. His knee injury was serious enough for him to retire from the game. He was only 22, which was a great shame.

In addition, the hat-trick in that match turned out to be the last goals that John Hannah would score for Darlington. He made only two more appearances before losing his place to Mark Forster. Forster had spent the summer playing in Sweden on loan and returned in mid-October. Hannah slipped further down the pecking order later that month when Knowles signed Garry MacDonald from Carlisle as he continued to reshape his squad. He joined Mark Miller in Malta as the pair tried their luck abroad. Personally, I'd have kept him as he certainly had something different to offer at the time.

EXETER CITY V DARLINGTON – 1984/85

One of many games that spring to mind from 1984/85 was Exeter City away at the end of October. Let me explain.

Barry went to the railway station to negotiate a reduction in the price of the train fare for a party booking since there were only 17 fans wanting to make the epic journey to St James Park. After a lot of discussion, he managed to negotiate a significant reduction for each person, which I have to say was great.

On the day in question, our numbers were further depleted when we realised that one lad, called Darren was missing from the group as the train pulled out of Bank Top station. 'Maybe he changed his mind at the last minute,' I suggested.

When we arrived at Exeter, Barry informed me that he wanted to look around the cathedral, which, fortunately or unfortunately whichever way you look at it, was only a short distance from the station. I must admit that going on an impromptu sightseeing tour was hardly at the top of my list of priorities. To be truthful, as he pushed me through the nave, I was like Andy from the TV comedy *Little Britain*, bored out of my mind and gagging for a drink.

Anyway, back to the real purpose behind our mammoth train journey. The game itself was certainly an eventful affair. Fred Barber saved a seventh-minute penalty. Then our debutant Garry MacDonald, signed from Carlisle United, scored with a tame shot from the edge of the area in the 34th minute. Exeter, though, equalised with seven minutes remaining.

However, just after Exeter had equalised, Stephen, who was also one of the 16, pointed at a lone figure trudging towards us and said, 'Isn't that Darren?' When Darren reached us, he explained that he'd slept in, caught a later train, knowing that it wouldn't arrive in time for the start of the game, and had paid full price for his ticket. Now there's true commitment for you!

After the match, the police dropped us off at the train station and then promptly left. Ten minutes later around 100 Exeter fans arrived at the scene. We were sitting there having a quiet cup of coffee when we heard one of them say, 'Let's get the one in the wheelchair!' All hell then broke loose. They chased the Darlington fans all over the platform, and regrettably, during the course of this skirmish, Stephen was slightly hurt. Another Darlo supporter called Bob was chased over the railway line. He was carrying some cans of lager in a plastic carrier bag and during the commotion they all fell out. An Exeter thug then bizarrely offered him two pence for his Darlington scarf, but he declined, whereupon the lad took it from him by force. Well, I suppose it would have made a good souvenir!

Finally, we caught the train back, having escaped from our encounter largely unscathed, apart from suffering a few cuts and bruises, arriving in Darlington well after midnight. As you might have guessed, during the long journey home I had to suffer the indignity of Stephen making fun of me for going to the cathedral, rather than the pub, with Barry.

PETERBOROUGH UNITED V DARLINGTON – 1984/85

A few weeks after my trip to Exeter, I went to London Road to see Peterborough v Darlington. Once again,

I went on the train with Barry, but this time on the understanding that we weren't going to visit any more cathedrals.

I vividly remember that we just happened to be walking past a town-centre pub during our pre-match booze cruise when, without warning, a stool came crashing through the window. Within seconds it was like one of those wild-west saloon brawls you see in the movies. To our amazement the two sets of fans stopped fighting to let us past; it was like pressing the pause button on a DVD player. As soon as we were out of the way, they carried on fighting as if nothing had happened. That incident stuck in my mind for months afterwards.

Anyway, some 400 Darlington fans had made the journey to London Road. Once we got inside the ground, it wasn't long before the violence flared up again. After two minutes, part of a small group of Darlington fans insisted on walking on the pitch as they were being ushered away from the home end. As the police were escorting them to the away enclosure, one of them was hit on the head with, of all things, a milk crate. The Darlington fans in the away end, incensed by this incident, scaled the perimeter fence and ran across the pitch towards the home fans. The game therefore had to be stopped for about five minutes so that mounted police could restore order and clear the pitch. Although Posh scored in the 45th minute, Dave McLean scored our equaliser direct from a corner late in the game.

The following Monday, the *Northern Echo*'s match report credited the home side's defender Martin Pike with an own goal. It was debatable, in fairness.

STOCKPORT COUNTY V DARLINGTON – 1984/85

The month after the Peterborough United match, Darlington played away at Stockport County. Unfortunately, Carl Airey, our leading goalscorer, was serving a two-match ban at the time and therefore missed this game.

For some unfathomable reason, Barry Weatherill committed the fatal mistake of putting me in charge of the supporters' club coach. Now that really was an error of judgement on his part. He even insisted that I shouldn't allow any alcohol on board, so to keep him happy, I promised that I wouldn't.

At this time, I should explain that there was a voluntary ban on alcohol on football coaches. Of course, my assurance that I wouldn't allow any booze on board was an exaggeration of the truth to say the very least – because the very first thing I did was to make sure that we went to an off-licence and got stocked up with cans of beer and lager. Not surprisingly, by the time we arrived at Stockport two hours later, everyone on the coach was the worse for wear; some more than others.

The game finished as an uneventful 0-0 draw on a frozen Edgeley Park pitch, a result that sent the Quakers to the top of the table. Darlo certainly missed Airey that night. Had he played, I think the away fans present would have witnessed a victory as Cyril Knowles's men were certainly toothless without him. Yet, not for the first time that season, they managed to grind out a point.

Despite it not being one of the best matches to watch, a good time was certainly had by everyone who travelled on the coach, especially Stephen, who accompanied me that night. He could hardly push me home and, much to my amusement, the normal 15-minute walk from Darlington town centre took him over an hour!

MIDDLESBROUGH V DARLINGTON – FA CUP THIRD ROUND 1984/85

On 5 January 1985, the Quakers were up against Middlesbrough at Ayresome Park in the third round of the FA Cup. I went to the match on the football special train service, again with Stephen.

Once in Middlesbrough, he pushed me along Linthorpe Road towards the ground, stopping off at a few pubs on the way. Although British Rail had laid on buses to the ground, there was no way that I could have got on board of one of those in my wheelchair.

On entering the ground, a couple of stewards gave Stephen a hand to carry me up into one of the seats in the home end. It was a bitterly cold afternoon and the pitch was covered in snow, while sleet showers drifted in from the North Sea.

While I was waiting for the game to start, I can remember thinking that this was always going to be a needle match because of the number of former Boro players in the Darlington squad. Apart from Cyril Knowles himself, there were seven with Boro connections: veteran full-back John Craggs, Peter Johnson, Phil Lloyd, Garry MacDonald, Mark Forster, Steve Tupling and Mick Angus.

Footballers revel in the knowledge that they might be able to put one over on their old club. Ironically, several of the Boro players who were part of their squad at that particular time later went on to play for the Quakers, including David Currie, Tony McAndrew, Alan Roberts and Paul Ward.

As for the game itself, I'm still convinced that Garry MacDonald scored a perfectly valid goal that day, but the referee adjudged that the ball hadn't crossed the line. Mick Saxby, the Boro defender, claimed to have hacked it away from the muddy goalmouth, but it was well over the line in my opinion.

Fred Barber played a blinder in the Darlo goal. One save that springs to mind was the point-blank stop he made towards the end of the match from the former Newcastle United defender Irving Nattress.

The 3,000 Darlo fans in the crowd of 19,084 went home happy, safe in the knowledge that they would have another crack at our near neighbours in the replay at Feethams.

DARLINGTON V MIDDLESBROUGH – FA CUP THIRD-ROUND REPLAY 1984/85

Three days later, Darlo played Middlesbrough in the replay after 50 or so loyal fans had turned up to clear the two inches of snow from the pitch. Because of the demand for tickets, Stephen stood in the Tin Shed and I had to go in one of the East Stand seats with Barry – my usual spot in the paddock wouldn't have afforded much of a view with so many bodies in front of me.

Spurred on by a crowd of 14,237, both sides tried to play football on a treacherous bog of a pitch, but the first half ended in a goalless stalemate.

However, things changed in the 53rd minute when Garry MacDonald managed to scramble the ball past the visiting goalkeeper Kelham O'Hanlon to put the Quakers 1-0 up. Feethams erupted. Cyril Knowles's men doubled their lead in the 76th minute. Darlington won a corner, Mitch Cook crossed into the box and Mike Angus rolled the ball through the muddy goalmouth to Phil Lloyd who toe-poked it into the net. Once more there was uproar but this time the Middlesbrough fans invaded the pitch in a vain attempt to get the game abandoned. The match was held up for ten minutes and the referee made it clear that if necessary he would wait until midnight to finish the game. I have to admit that the violence was pretty bad but the police managed to eventually bring it under control. Altogether there were 15 arrests and three people were taken to hospital. Concrete slabs and iron spikes were even hurled at the police after a 20-yard section of the perimeter fencing behind one of the goals collapsed.

After what seemed like an eternity, the game was restarted and Tony McAndrew almost instantly pulled a goal back for Boro. Darlo therefore had to endure a frantic last ten minutes before the referee blew the final whistle. I was ecstatic with what was an outstanding victory.

The Boro fans, by contrast, were still seething at the indignity of their defeat by a lower-division team and some of them vented their anger on the perimeter fencing and vandalised the cricket pitch on their way out of the ground. They actually fought a running battle with the Darlo fans on the cricket pitch, which spilled out into the town centre. I also heard later that they set a railway carriage on fire as they made their way home, ripping out the seats and smashing the light fittings. The fire brigade were consequently called out to Middlesbrough railway station. They were certainly sore losers that night.

BURY V DARLINGTON – 1984/85

A couple of months after the Middlesbrough game, I went to Bury for the evening fixture with Barry in his car along with two of the directors' wives. We arrived at the ground at about six o'clock. The two women preferred to head for the directors' box, while Barry and I went drinking in Bury town centre instead.

When we returned to Gigg Lane in time for the kick-off, the pair of us were shocked to discover that it was pitch-dark inside the ground because there was a problem with the electricity supply. Even though the floodlights were working, no doubt because they were powered by a separate generator, the scene in the bar was a different story – an old woman was faffing about in the till, looking for loose change, with her only source of light some flickering candles.

Unfortunately, Barry and I were separated as we entered the ground and on this occasion I was put in the home end by a steward.

During the first half, a drunken Bury fan decided to throw a punch at me. Although I managed to duck, I lost my balance in the process and fell out of my wheelchair. Within a few seconds a dozen thugs were putting the boot into me. When the Darlington fans saw what was happening they ran across the pitch towards me. There I was, lying on the terraces, with a battle going on all around me. It was a frightening experience and one I'll never forget since it left me nursing two cracked ribs.

To add to my woes, when Andy Hill scored the only goal of the match for the Shakers in the 68th minute, Darlo had their lead at the top of the table reduced to two points.

After the game, Barry and the two directors' wives were shocked by the severity of my injuries and as a precaution I went to Darlington Memorial Hospital on my return for a check-up where my cracked ribs were strapped up.

Although I could have pressed charges against the hooligan who assaulted me, I decided not to.

Being in pain for some time after what had happened to me wasn't the sort of thing that was going to stop me from travelling to see my team in action. My mother pleaded with me not to go anymore, but I was determined not to let the hooligans win. Moreover, even the disappointing result couldn't shake my belief in my beloved Darlo.

CREWE ALEXANDRA V DARLINGTON – 1984/85

In May 1985, I went to Crewe for the last away game of the season. Prior to this match, Cyril Knowles's men needed a point in order to clinch promotion.

Once the supporters' club coach arrived at Feethams, Gavin kindly lifted me on board because Stephen had broken his leg playing football a few days before in Darlington's South Park.

However, despite having his leg in plaster up to his thigh, he still managed to push my wheelchair to the ground, which was quite a feat of dexterity on his part.

This was also the first game I went to with Ian Carter, who was destined to become a very close friend, and remains so to this day.

Carl Airey scored both our goals, on five and then 25 minutes, to bring his tally to 18 for the season, and in between times Kevan Smith got on the scoresheet after

15 minutes, albeit at the wrong end. David Waller scored the equaliser for Crewe in the 85th minute. Interestingly, I should add that David Platt, who later went on to play for England, starred for the Railwaymen that night. All this meant that my beloved Quakers had secured the point they had needed and would be playing in the Third Division the following season.

As a matter of interest, I had a massive Darlington flag with me and I waved it for the whole of the first half. By that time my arms were killing me so I talked Ian into waving it for me. I kept telling him to hold it higher and by the end of the match he could hardly move his arms.

At the end of the game, having clinched promotion, all the players threw their shirts into the crowd. I caught Mark Forster's (Mark had previously promised to throw his in my direction) but some moron wrenched it out of my hand and it was gone. Strangely enough, some 14 years later, I bumped into Mark at a Darlington FC reunion. In the course of our conversation, I happened to mention this incident. When he heard my tale, he promised to give me a signed shirt from the 1984/85 season. True to his word, he posted the shirt through my letterbox the following day. From that day on, we became firm friends, and have remained so ever since.

Stephen, with the pot on his leg, climbed the fence to get a better view of the celebrations. I can still see him now, hanging by one leg, absolutely lapping up the occasion. Ian lifted me up too so that I could see what was happening on the pitch, but unfortunately while I was standing up some nice person stole the programme from my seat. It took me many years to secure a replacement and even then I had to pay £20 for it.

The final memory from that night is of Stephen, Ian and I sitting in a service station, halfway between Crewe and Darlington, eating a meal, when there was a sudden roar: the Darlington team bus had stopped there as well.

Everyone started singing and Cyril Knowles came over and had a long chat with me. We spoke about the game and about the season as a whole. That is the thing I loved about Cyril – he would always chat to the fans after matches.

The players themselves were mobbed by the fans and they spent three or four hours just talking and signing autographs. They all had time to come and talk to the supporters because they knew how much it meant to them. Some players don't have time for the fans, and that's sad. Looking back, I can honestly say most of the 1984/85 squad always spoke to me after matches, which was great. Indeed, captain Kevan Smith and striker Mark Forster are still good friends of mine to this day.

I remember that I went home thinking, 'I'm only 20 and I've seen us get promotion whereas some people have supported the club for years and have seen only mediocrity.' The previous time we were promoted from the old Fourth Division was in 1965/66 when we finished level on points with Doncaster Rovers. On this occasion we ended up third, one point behind Blackpool. It had certainly been a long wait for some.

YORK CITY V DARLINGTON – 1985/86

Having been promoted to the Third Division, Darlo soon found out that this would prove a greater test of our mettle, especially now that we were without the services of Kevan Smith to shore up our defence after he had been sold to Rotherham in the close-season. Not surprisingly, by the time we played York City at Bootham Crescent in October 1985 we were already bottom of the table.

As a matter of interest, in the early hours of the Saturday morning prior to the match, vandals had managed to get into the ground and broke the crossbar of one of the goals. This, however, didn't stop the match from going ahead.

Before heading to the game, Darlington fans went on the rampage in York city centre, smashing windows and brawling. Trouble also flared up during the match and altogether there were 30 arrests for public order offences that day.

Stephen, Ian, Malcolm and Clare (a couple who came with us to matches for a while) and I made the half-hour trip to York by train. I remember that we arrived there at 11 o'clock; in other words, opening time. I got absolutely plastered. After a few pints, we went to a quite posh restaurant in the city centre for a meal. Once inside, I noticed a woman wearing a hat with artificial fruit on it, sat at another table. I couldn't help singing, 'Where did you get that hat, where did you get that hat?' only to be roundly rebuked by my friends, but by then I was past caring.

Following the meal, we resumed our pub crawl, and by the time we got to the ground I was totally out of it. Because of my state, the game just became an alcoholic blur. I later found out that Paul Ward was sent off for the Quakers in the 24th minute, York City's Tony Canham scored a hat-trick and Keith Walwyn (now sadly deceased) got two. Steve Senior (who had been on loan with us the previous season) and Keith Houchen also chipped in with a goal apiece, making a grand total of seven.

After the match, I honestly thought that we had won 7-0, not the other way around! All the lads were naturally devastated by the result and there I was laughing. One of them said, 'Paul, what are you laughing at?' So, I told him that it was because we'd won 7-0. He replied, 'You daft bastard, we lost 7-0. Which match have you been watching?'

DERBY COUNTY V DARLINGTON – 1985/86

In March 1986, I made the trip to title favourites Derby County with Ian in Clare and Malcolm's car.

Once in the ground, we witnessed a battling Darlington performance with central defenders John Green and Peter Robinson managing to tame the potent Derby strike force of Bobby Davison and Trevor Christie, although the latter did score in the 25th minute. Unfortunately, Green was eventually led from the field and substituted in the 59th minute after a clash of heads with Davison. A minute later Carl Airey touched on a free kick to Paul Ward who hammered it into the net to earn the Quakers a creditable 1-1 draw.

Another interesting fact from that match was that Steve Tupling was bizarrely sent off in the third minute of injury time for retaliation against John Gregory, who would later become manager of Aston Villa, before returning to Derby County.

This was my first (and only) visit to the Baseball Ground. I have to say, it was hard to believe that Derby were in the third tier of English football at that particular time, given the facilities and players they had at their disposal. This, in my opinion, showed two things: firstly, so-called 'big clubs' shouldn't take their status for granted. Manchester City, Leeds United, Sunderland, Sheffield Wednesday, Middlesbrough, Wolverhampton Wanderers and several other clubs have found themselves in the lower reaches of the Football League at some time in their history. So, it can happen to anyone. Secondly, achieving a draw showed how good Darlington were on that particular day. In fact, that season, the Quakers actually ended up taking four points out of six off Derby, beating them 2-1 at Feethams the following May with goals from

Dave McLean and Carl Airey. Phil Gee netted for the visitors that night.

YORK CITY V DARLINGTON – 1986/87

Our first match of the 1986/87 season was away at York City. I went there on the train with Ian, Malcolm and Clare. On this occasion I stayed sober, not wanting to repeat my experience of my previous visit to Bootham Crescent. Stephen travelled up from London (he had relocated to the capital during that summer to look for work) and met us at York station for a game in which David Currie, signed from Middlesbrough in the close-season, and former Grimsby player Mark Hine made their debuts.

Derek Hood scored first for the Minstermen from the penalty spot in the 17th minute after Phil Lloyd was adjudged to have handled the ball. However, when Tony Canham scored their second goal on the stroke of half-time he appeared to be yards offside, but the linesman didn't raise his flag, so I turned my attention to Viv Busby, the York City coach, who by that time was jumping up and down celebrating the goal and said he must be blind to think that the goal was onside. But he was adamant that it was and ignored my protests. Incidentally, afterwards, the press interviewed Denis Smith, the York manager, and he admitted that it *was* offside, after all.

Returning to the match, Tony Ford added a third for York in the 55th minute before David Currie scored a consolation goal 11 minutes from time.

Ian, Stephen and I all agreed that Darlo were well-beaten on the day and that judging by that performance, unless several additions were made to the squad, they'd go down. We also agreed that Carl Airey and Dave McLean, who had left at the end of the previous season, would be a huge miss. This turned out to be true, as the team struggled to both score and indeed create goals that season.

SWINDON TOWN V DARLINGTON 1986/87

In March 1987, Cyril Knowles was unfairly sacked as Darlo manager and replaced with Paul Ward, who took on the role of caretaker player-manager. At the age of 24, Ward was, and still remains, the youngest ever manager in Football League history. I had always liked Cyril, and kept in touch with him until his death a few years later.

One story that springs to mind is that when Torquay United took the decision to ban all away fans in the late 1980s, Cyril, who by then was their manager, rang me and invited me, Ian and two other Quakers fans to their game against Darlington as his guests. We all went in Ian's car. On arrival at the ground, Cyril invited us to his office for a drink. I never forgot that act of kindness, as it was something that he didn't have to do, but he made the effort to do so.

A word about Paul Ward; I first met him in 1985 and, 36 years later, we remain in contact and are good friends. Over the years, he has helped me out with many charity matches, for which I'm extremely grateful.

Anyway, back to the game in question. In April 1987 my friend John Gray and I decided to hire a Ford Sierra to go to Swindon for this rearranged midweek fixture.

Unfortunately, the two other people who were supposed to be sharing the costs cancelled at the last minute, which meant that the two of us had to shell out nearly £60 each to cover the cost of hiring the car, which was a lot of money then. Not only that, but we also missed the kick-off because John decided to stop off at a well-known fish and chip shop called the Wetherby Whaler for something to eat.

Although we lost 1-0, we played some excellent football, with our goalkeeper Jeremy Roberts and the defensive partnership of Gary Hinchley and Phil Lloyd particularly outstanding. This was a game where the defenders were under constant pressure and it came as no real surprise when Bryan Wade scored for the home side in the 90th minute. Lloyd tried desperately to clear the ball, but after the linesman flagged and the referee awarded the goal.

Nevertheless, it was the return journey that proved to be memorable. When we stopped at a pub, John inadvertently locked the keys in the car, so we had to get one of the locals who was drinking in the same pub to open the door with a bent coat hanger, which took him ages.

On the way back, John was feeling tired so we stopped for a rest at a service station. He was having a power nap while I read the matchday programme and listened to the radio. We were just sitting in the car when all of a sudden, out of the blackness, two police cars surrounded us with blue lights flashing, like something out of *The Bill*. For some reason they thought we were car thieves and they therefore ordered us both to get out. I explained that I was disabled. They were still a bit dubious even when John opened the boot and showed them my wheelchair, but eventually they let us go, allowing us to complete our journey home without further incident.

CHESTERFIELD V DARLINGTON – 1986/87

By the time Darlington visited Chesterfield in May 1987, we had already been relegated to the Fourth Division. Ian and I made the journey with Clare and Malcolm in their car.

Quite an annoying incident happened that day which taught me a lot about human nature. Let me explain. Prior to the match, a Darlington player gave Malcolm a wad of complimentary tickets to hand out to the visiting fans. However, rather than do just that, he took two out (for him and Clare) and then, to my amazement, proceeded to rip up the rest. Malcolm simply threw the shredded pieces of paper on the pavement and said, 'I can't be arsed waiting about to give these away.' I piped up and responded by stating, 'Ian and I would have liked a couple of those tickets.' Malcolm replied, 'I'm sorry, I didn't think.' This comment amazed Ian and I and showed the worst side of a person. If Malcolm had given the tickets to us, we'd have happily hung around near the turnstiles and handed them out to the Quakers fans who had made the trip for a pointless match.

At that moment, we both decided not to travel with them again as this was the last in a long line of selfish and indeed greedy acts that neither of us felt comfortable with.

To add to our woes, Tony Coyle drilled a right-footed shot from the edge of the area low into the bottom corner in the second minute. It was the only goal of the game. The only noteworthy event from my point of view was that Dale Anderson, a 16-year-old trainee, became the youngest ever player that day to represent Darlington. Over 20 years later, Curtis Main took the mantle away from him when he made his debut at the tender age of 15, against Peterborough United. One final comment about Dale – I met him at an event, we got chatting and we became firm friends, so much so that we remain in regular contact, and have remained firm friends to this day.

HALIFAX TOWN V DARLINGTON – 1987/88

The summer of 1987 saw David Booth take over as Darlington manager. The former Grimsby boss had been out of the game for a couple of years but was chosen as the man to get Darlington back on track.

The club was preparing for life back in the Fourth Division after two seasons in the Third Division under Cyril Knowles and then Paul Ward.

One of Booth's first acts was to appoint Phil Bonnyman as his assistant. The 33-year-old Scottish midfielder was signed from Grimsby and had previously played for Hamilton, Carlisle and Chesterfield. He would provide valuable experience to the Quakers' midfield, as well as his coaching responsibilities. The new manager also added Huddersfield Town striker Gary Worthington, nephew of the more famous Frank, full-back Mark Outterside from Sunderland, winger Kevin Stonehouse (now sadly deceased) from Blackpool and central defender Dave McAughtrie from York City to his squad in preparation for the new campaign.

I was actually quite optimistic for the new season as I boarded the train with Ian for Darlington's first fixture of 1987/88, which was away at Halifax Town.

When we arrived at York station, we got off the train and waited for half an hour or so for our connecting service to Halifax.

However, once on board, we were dismayed to find that we were in the company of an old tramp who had one of those shopping trolleys with him that seem to be the preserve of old-age pensioners. His was one of the dirtiest, smelliest individuals that I'd ever seen, and rather than move it round me he proceeded to put it right over my legs. Then, catching sight of me, he said, 'What the hell have you done to yourself? You must be a freak of nature, boy.' Given his own grotesque appearance, the irony of this remark seemed to have escaped him entirely. Ian, though, thought his comment was hilarious and called me 'a freak of nature' for months afterwards.

When we arrived in Halifax we met Stephen at the station and the three of us went to a pub called The Shay, which was named after Halifax's ground. While in there, the three of us discussed an article in that day's *Northern Echo* which quoted chairman Archie Heaton, who stated that the club was in a precarious financial position due to the low gates at Feethams. Reflecting on the story, we agreed that if the team played better football they would get more people through the turnstiles and generate more revenue. Ian, however, pointed out that this was a vicious circle, as to strengthen the squad significantly would require spending money which the club simply didn't have. Thinking about it, both arguments were right, making it an impossible situation.

Once inside the ground, we witnessed a good first-half performance by the Quakers. In the eighth minute Mark Hine passed the ball through to Garry MacDonald who rolled it underneath the advancing Halifax keeper, Paddy Roche, the former Ireland and Manchester United stopper, to give Darlo the lead.

The second half was a different story. After defender Gary Hinchley went off injured, the visitors lost their shape and their defence started to struggle. Halifax manager Billy Ayre, the former Hartlepool defender, must have noticed this and brought on substitutes Wayne Allison and Neil Matthews. This proved to be a turning point in the game. Shortly afterwards, Allison equalised for the first time. Despite David Currie restoring Darlo's one-goal advantage seconds later, our joy was short-lived when Matthews netted Halifax's equaliser seconds before the final whistle to give the Shaymen a share of the points. This was the first time in their history that both substitutes had come off the bench and scored. An interesting fact I thought I'd share with the reader.

YORK CITY V DARLINGTON – FREIGHT ROVER TROPHY – 1987/88

In October 1987, I went to York with Ian by car for a Freight Rover Trophy tie.

In the disabled area, there happened to be an absolute idiot of a York City fan sitting beside us who managed to get on both our nerves. Since on rare occasions when I'm provoked, I can be one of the most obnoxious people alive, Ian warned me, 'For God's sake, Paul, just ignore him,' so I agreed I'd be on my best behaviour. But this lad went droning on and on about his knowledge of football and the offside law in particular, and he was just talking rubbish as far as the two of us were concerned.

So, in the end, Ian, who could bear it no longer, turned to him and said, 'Will you shut the f*** up?' As you can imagine I ribbed Ian about that outburst later, especially after all the lecturing he had given me about being well behaved.

Anyway, to the match in question, although Darlington started the match brightly, hitting the post twice, the home side took the lead in the 18th minute totally against the run of play. However, seven minutes later the Quakers drew level through David Currie. Darlo then went in front through Peter Robinson in the 38th minute before Dale Banton netted an equaliser in the 53rd minute. A minute later, though, Paul Ward regained our one-goal advantage.

Then came the turning point in the game when our keeper Paul Crichton, who was later to play for York, limped off the pitch with an injury to be replaced in goal by midfielder Phil Bonnyman.

With an outfield player between the sticks, it was always going to be difficult to hang on to our lead and in the 69th minute Alan Whitehead levelled for the home side. Credit to Darlo, they kept battling away and in the 81st minute Garry MacDonald popped up to notch a fourth and winning goal for the visitors. Despite the Minstermen piling on the pressure, including pushing centre-half Steve Tutill (later to play for Darlo) up front, David Booth's men held on to their lead to register a dramatic 4-3 victory.

Ian's altercation with the York fan was certainly not the only flashpoint of the game, as Booth was called out of the dugout by the referee, Ken Redfern, for remarks he made, and warned that if he repeated them he'd have to sit in the stand. All in all, it was a typical derby game, full of passion and commitment, but above all it was a win, which made the journey back home in Ian's car all the sweeter.

DARLINGTON V EXETER CITY – 1987/88

By the time Exeter City visited Feethams at the beginning of December, the Quakers sat 12th in the table, with a record of seven wins and seven defeats from their 19 games, with 30 goals scored and 30 conceded. I went to this game with Ian. We sat in the East Stand paddock together.

Exeter were originally scheduled to visit Feethams on Saturday, 28 November, but that game had been controversially postponed less than an hour before kick-off due to a frozen pitch. The referee had delayed his decision as long as possible to allow the aforementioned pitch to thaw. The game was rearranged for ten days later on Tuesday, 8 December, and as people arrived at the ground there were fears of another postponement due to the frozen conditions.

Spectators who'd been inside the ground on the original date claimed that the pitch was in a worse state for the rearrangement. The rumour around the ground was that Exeter had insisted that the game go ahead, so they wouldn't have another wasted trip. Because of the freezing temperatures and a general feeling that the match wouldn't take place, only 1,107 hardy souls turned out.

They were rewarded with a one-sided encounter as Darlington secured their best home win of the season, inspired by a brilliant individual performance from David Currie, whom the Exeter defence found completely unplayable on the icy surface. Darlo were ahead as early as the third minute. Garry MacDonald made progress down the wing and played the ball inside to Mark Hine, who drove the ball across visiting keeper John Shaw and inside the far post. Eight minutes later it was nearly two as a Peter Robinson back header from an Alan Roberts corner was cleared off the line by Ray Carter.

The one-way traffic continued and Kevin Stonehouse was the next to go close in the 17th minute when he crashed a header against the bar after a superb chip by Currie. Then it was MacDonald's turn as he saw his header blocked on the line, before Shaw made a brilliant double save to keep out his follow-up effort and also one from Roberts. Darlington continued to pour forward and increased their lead in the 37th minute when Currie latched on to a Hine through ball and calmly side-footed past Shaw's despairing dive. Three minutes later Currie made it 3-0 with the goal of the game. Receiving the ball wide on the left, he cut inside two defenders and unleashed a powerful drive past the helpless keeper from just outside the box.

The total domination continued after the break and on the hour Currie turned provider to set up the fourth goal. He skated past Richard Massey to the byline and crossed for Roberts to smash home from two yards out. Exeter grabbed a consolation goal in the 77th minute when Simon Mitton prodded home following a goalmouth scramble but they finished the match a well-beaten side. They never came to terms with the icy surface and couldn't handle Currie, whose balance and tricky skills seemed unaffected by the frozen conditions. I can remember saying to Ian as he pushed me home that I thought we'd go up if we managed to keep hold of our star striker.

SCUNTHORPE UNITED V DARLINGTON – 1987/88

On Boxing Day 1987, the Quakers played away at Scunthorpe United. Ian and I travelled there in a transit van with some other lads and since we arrived into the town centre for opening time, he pushed my wheelchair straight into the nearest pub.

Consequently, by ten to three we were both rather the worse for wear as we entered the away end of the now demolished Old Show Ground.

Given our bleary-eyed demeanour, we were hardly in a fit state to marvel at the imposing glass and steel architecture of the club's East Stand. This strikingly modern design was actually opened in 1958 and was the first cantilever football stand in the country.

To be honest, I was surprised the stewards on the gate let us in the stadium, but as we entered I remember Ian commenting, 'I'm sure there's a step around here somewhere, we nearly tripped over it last yeaaargh …' Bang! He couldn't have timed it better and I was catapulted out of my chair. Luckily a steward and a policeman came to our assistance and rushed the two of us to the St John Ambulance first-aid tent. The policeman then asked Ian, 'Have you been drinking, young man?' Ian, who could hardly stagger, let alone stand up straight, said, 'No, I haven't touched a drop, officer.' The policeman turned a blind eye, but I'll never forget that reply from Ian; it was indeed a classic!

To our great surprise, we managed to get into the away end where we witnessed a pretty poor first half. However, in the first few minutes David Currie had a rasping shot finger-tipped on to the bar by goalkeeper Martin Taylor, on loan from Derby County. Unfortunately for the visitors, only three minutes after Currie's effort, Andy Flounders took advantage of slack marking at the far post to shoot past Jeremy Roberts in the Darlo goal.

The game then petered out into a dour midfield battle, by which time Ian and I were both bored out of our brains and looking forward to our next pint. Darlo rallied for a final flourish in the last 15 minutes when Currie hit the foot of the post after turning two home defenders inside out. Mark Hine also had a point-blank header saved on the line by Taylor. But it wasn't to be our day and the Iron ran out 1-0 winners.

The following Monday I was quite amused to read the *Northern Echo*'s description of the game in which the newspaper said it was about as appetising as a 'third helping of cold Christmas turkey'. I couldn't have put it better myself.

SCARBOROUGH V DARLINGTON – 1988/89

In October 1988, Darlington played Scarborough away, still not having registered a single league victory that season. Before Ian and I caught the local train service to Scarborough we had to change at York, so we decided to go for a few pints in the city centre. My entourage that day comprised Ian, Phil Rutter (who is from Darlington) and two lads from Sheffield called Brian Elsey and Trevor Rutter (no relation to Phil), who are both originally from the Darlington area.

A week before the Scarborough match, I'd been talking to Ian about the song 'Billy, Don't Be a Hero' by the group Paper Lace. Coincidentally, the song was playing on the pub jukebox. So, for a laugh, the lads decided to bind me hand and foot to my wheelchair with their scarves and made me sing the song, word for word, before they would untie me. I didn't care; I don't even particularly like the song, but fortunately I managed to remember all the words, so I was released. The whole scene was highly amusing in fairness. We did, however, get some funny looks from the pub regulars.

That day, Darlington had so many injuries that one of our forwards, Garry MacDonald, played in defence. Craig Short scored for Scarborough in the 21st minute and Steve Norris added a second in the 35th. Mark Hine then hit a 20-yard drive that went in off the underside of the crossbar to pull a goal back for the Quakers. Paul Emson then scored an equaliser with a low shot from 15 yards in the 76th minute. But with only six minutes left, Norris hit Scarborough's winner, meaning that Darlo were still waiting for their first league victory. I can remember saying to Ian as we left the ground that we were relegation fodder. He agreed that I could be right.

Unfortunately, my worst fears came true and striker David Currie was sold to Barnsley for a paltry £150,000 in February 1988. His replacement, Paul Clayton, a then record £20,000 signing from Norwich City, failed to live up to expectations, despite scoring two goals on his debut against Crewe Alexandra. Without the goals of their talisman, the Quakers' form slumped dramatically, and this carried on into the following season.

COLCHESTER UNITED V DARLINGTON – 1988/89

On 25 November 1988, I went with Ian to Layer Road, for a game against Colchester United, who were our nearest rivals in our battle to avoid relegation to the GM Vauxhall Conference. We travelled on the supporters' coach, setting off at about nine in the morning. When we arrived at the ground we went to their supporters' club bar, which was up a flight of stairs. Ian and some other lads lifted me up in my wheelchair.

From a window you could see out over the pitch. I said to Ian, 'This game is never going to go ahead.' Thick fog rolling in from the North Sea made visibility very difficult for the sparse crowd of only 1,550. The referee gave the go-ahead only half an hour before the game was due to start.

Inside the ground we met up with Stephen Lowson and saw John Gray and Richard Jones, who were also there. Prior to kick-off, a steward informed us that the referee was insisting that it was no good having fans behind any of the goals due to the poor visibility. Instead, everyone was moved to the Main Stand. Ian carried me up to one of the wooden bench seats.

Even so, from my vantage point I couldn't see either set of goalposts. Nevertheless, despite the atrocious conditions, Gary Worthington scored a penalty for the Quakers in the 25th minute, then added a second in the 63rd minute with Mark Radford scoring Colchester's consolation goal in the 72nd minute.

After the game I spoke to Phil Bonnyman, who was naturally pleased with the result. This was Darlington's second successive away win, which hauled them off the bottom of the table. We then had a few celebratory drinks in Colchester before we caught a train back to London where we were staying at Stephen's house.

SCUNTHORPE UNITED V DARLINGTON – 1988/89

The penultimate game of the 1988/89 season was away to Scunthorpe United on 6 May, and we desperately needed to win to avoid relegation to the Conference.

Brian Little had taken over from the likeable Dave Booth in February 1989 and, while results improved slightly, the Quakers remained deep in relegation trouble, as they had done throughout that fateful season. I have to say, the team were awful that season and without doubt they deserved to be at the bottom of the league when Little arrived.

Anyway, Ian picked me up at my flat in his car at about ten in the morning. As we drove towards Humberside, we were both quite optimistic about our chances of surviving the drop and saw plenty of fans in cars and coaches making the same journey as us.

We arrived in Scunthorpe at about midday and parked in the car park of the Berkeley pub near the ground. We then went for a drink where we mingled with the home and away fans.

Ian then pushed me the short distance to the ground where we paid our entrance money. We both shelled out 60 pence for a programme, perhaps with the thought in the back of our minds that this might be our last Football League encounter for many years.

This was my first visit to Scunthorpe's new Glanford Park stadium: its breeze block and corrugated-iron structure was more reminiscent of a cattle market than a football ground. However, the disabled facilities were adequate which was all that one could ask for I suppose.

Once inside the ground, I soon realised the enormity of the match. 'The Darlo's stayin' up, the Darlo's stayin' up. Now you're gonna believe us, now you're gonna believe us, now you're gonna believe us, the Darlo's stayin' up!' The 700 or so supporters behind me kept up this optimistic chant for most of the first half.

However, by half-time we were already 1-0 down, though it certainly wasn't a case of one-way traffic. Paul Musselwhite, Scunthorpe's goalkeeper, was fortunate to tip a Garry MacDonald header on to his post. But after a 12-minute spell in the second half, we were 5-0 down, with Tony Daws scoring a hat-trick. The only bright spot was an 80th-minute goal from Paul Willis (now no longer with us) from fully 40 yards.

The final scoreline of 5-1 to the home side ensured that Darlo were relegated to the Conference. Brian Little, despite the relegation, would later become one of our most successful postwar managers. As I mentioned above, the team was very poor and he was on a hiding to nothing from the minute he walked through the door. David Cork, who would later sign for us and spearhead our push for promotion the following season, played for the Iron that day.

I'll certainly never forget the emotion after the game. Ian and I were in tears along with many other grown men and women. Yet, despite having suffered such a crushing defeat, the fans shouted for the team to come back out on the field, which they did. Garry MacDonald came over to apologise in person and threw his shirt into the crowd. Even the Scunthorpe United fans commiserated with us and sang in comradely fashion, 'You'll be back, you'll be back.'

But it was what happened afterwards that stands out for me. During the journey back home, Ian and I were silent, totally absorbed in our own thoughts. We didn't speak to each other at all. It was like having suffered bereavement. In fact, Ian seemed to be driving in a trance.

Anyway, we made it back to Colburn, near Catterick Garrison, in just under an hour and a quarter. We arrived at Ian's local pub, the Colburn Lodge, at about a quarter past six. However, none of the customers believed that we'd been to the match. They all thought we were lying. So as proof we showed them our programmes.

FARNBOROUGH TOWN V DARLINGTON – 1989/90

After I had recovered from the seismic shock to my nervous system brought on by our relegation to the

Conference, life as a Darlington supporter became more bearable following our terrific start to the new season as we went 11 games unbeaten.

In November 1989 Ian and I travelled on the train to our away game at Farnborough Town. Having both already consumed several cans en route, by the time we met Stephen at King's Cross we were pretty inebriated. Despite this, we couldn't resist having some more to drink in Coopers Bar in the station.

After three or four pints, we caught a train from Liverpool Street to Farnborough, a place which is arguably more famous for its air show than its football team. We found a pub just outside the station where we had a few more pints and then went up a steep hill to another one, which was heaving with Darlo fans. A little old man who must have been about 80 years old and was wearing a hearing aid was serving behind the bar. Naturally, the Darlo fans were giving him grief by singing, 'Why are we waiting?' and 'Beer beer, we want more beer!' as he struggled to cope with the sheer number of people wanting a drink. After having a pint, neither Ian nor Stephen fancied queuing again, so we left and went somewhere different.

Around 30 minutes before the game was due to start, we entered the supporters' club bar of the John Roberts Ground. After a quick pint, one of the club officials kindly opened a door leading to the stands, which effectively meant that we were allowed to get into the ground free of charge. I cheekily made a remark to the effect that it must have been my birthday.

Darlo were four points clear at the top of the table at that time and Farnborough had lost six at home already, so on paper it should have been an easy three points for Brian Little's men. However, as I'd learned over the years, football isn't as black and white as that. This again proved to be true as in the 62nd minute the home side scored through Roddy Braithwaite as a result of a sloppy back-pass by Kevan Smith, who had returned to the club that summer, and this proved to be the only goal of the game.

It just goes to show, there's no such thing as a 'banker' in football; Darlington's result at Farnborough proved that beyond doubt.

CHELTENHAM TOWN V DARLINGTON – 1989/90

At the time Ian and I travelled to Cheltenham on the supporters' coach in December 1989, Darlo were still top of the table.

History was about to be made – this was the first meeting between Darlington and Cheltenham, so it was my first visit to their ground.

Having left Feethams at about eight in the morning, we stopped off at the Trowell service station near Nottingham before we made our way to Cheltenham, arriving there at about one o'clock.

When our driver pulled into a superstore car park near the Robins' Whaddon Road ground, the police ordered all the supporters to stay on board the coach.

Since I had no intention of remaining on the coach, I told a little white lie and said that I had to get off and empty my catheter bag.

Just to confirm, I'm not fitted with a catheter at all, I just use a plastic bottle if I need to urinate, but the police weren't to know that. So, a kindly officer let Ian get me off the coach and we went for four or five pints in two or three different pubs (in one of those pubs we met Stephen, who later accompanied us to the match) while the remaining supporters stayed put. This was one of those very rare occasions when being disabled had its advantages!

The game itself was a scrappy affair, a situation that wasn't helped by the blustery wind and driving rain. Cheltenham had signed Andy Gray, the former Aston Villa and Scotland striker, from Glasgow Rangers during the close season, but he limped off four minutes into the second half. In any event, his impact on the game had been very minimal – if memory serves me right, he did nothing but mouth off to the referee and moan at his team-mates.

Although Les McJannet was harshly sent off for the Quakers in the 24th minute, we still won 1-0 thanks to an 82nd-minute goal from flying winger Paul Emson. So it was a good day all round. Stephen simply couldn't contain his excitement and, before we could stop him, he had easily hurdled the low perimeter fence as he attempted to sprint across the pitch to congratulate the goalscorer. But because of the heavy ground he couldn't catch our winger, so he eventually gave up and rejoined the crowd. Fortunately, Stephen's rush of blood occurred in more enlightened times when a fan who strayed on to the pitch wasn't liable to be bundled away by stewards and banned for life.

Cheltenham struck me as quite an unlikely hotbed of football. Although the team was sponsored by Gulf Oil, who had their headquarters in the town, the programme only reinforced my initial impression: the front-cover photograph sported a fine row of elegant Regency houses and beautifully tended flowerbeds. More like Harrogate, in fact, than places I was used to visiting, such as Hartlepool!

RUNCORN V DARLINGTON – 1989/90

Three days after my trip to Cheltenham, I visited Runcorn. Now this was more like the kind of place you'd expect a football team to flourish: a gritty northern industrial town near the Manchester Ship Canal.

It was a bitterly cold December evening when Ian picked me up in his car after work and we made the relatively short journey to Cheshire.

We arrived at about seven with only time for a swift half before we made our way to the ground where we

117

bumped into my good friend, and fellow Darlo fan, Steve Keeney.

As we approached the only turnstile to the ramshackle Canal Street ground, we had to negotiate what was in effect a ploughed field.

Once inside the stadium, Steve went to the refreshment kiosk to get us a cup of tea, only to find that the queue was a mile long. Not only that, but they were also using a small gas stove underneath a ten-gallon urn of ice-cold water in a vain attempt to bring it to the boil. Eventually, with the home side 2-0 up, Steve eventually managed to get served by the old dear on the counter. But when he handed over a 50-pence piece for a Mars bar she was so slow that she couldn't work out the correct change. I certainly laughed as he recounted the tale! It brought back memories of Bury away in 1984/85, which I spoke about earlier.

Anyway, given the freezing-cold weather and the liquid that I had consumed, it wasn't long before I had to ask Ian to take me to the gents' toilet. However, what we were confronted with had us both rubbing our eyes in disbelief.

Now I'm not suggesting it was dirty, quite the opposite, that distinction surely goes to the ladies' toilet at Rochdale, which I was forced to use on one occasion due to the fact that the gents were inaccessible. That particular toilet was truthfully the dirtiest and smelliest I'd ever seen in my life. It reminded me of a scene from

Trainspotting – you know the one I mean. No, what was so unusual about the gents' toilet at Runcorn was that it was only half-built. There was simply a breeze-block wall a few courses high to shelter me from the brass-monkey weather and to protect my modesty at the same time. Well, I suppose I should have been grateful that I could still watch the match from my vantage point, but unfortunately the result wasn't what I'd been hoping for because we went on to lose 2-1 with David Cork replying for the Quakers in what was a disappointing defeat.

NORTHWICH VICTORIA V DARLINGTON – 1989/90

The race for the title was still very much in the balance in March 1990 when Darlington played Northwich Victoria at their Drill Field ground.

Northwich Victoria were one of four former league sides in the Conference that season, alongside Darlington, Merthyr Tydfil and Barrow. In fact, they were founder members of the Second Division in 1892, but they only lasted for two seasons before they dropped out of the league in 1894, never to return.

This was our third meeting that season as we had already comprehensively beaten them 4-0 in the league and 6-2 in the first round of the FA Cup.

After I'd left work, my father dropped me off at Catterick Bridge, close to where Ian works. He then drove me the rest of the way and we parked in a side street near the ground, arriving just in time for the evening kick-off.

Unlike the previous two matches, this game was a brutal affair. The home side resorted to the most cynical tactics, which amounted to literally kicking our players off the pitch. There was even a rumour going around that the chairman of one of our promotion rivals had offered the Northwich players £1,000 per man to stop us from winning the game, though I should add that this was never actually substantiated.

In the 14th minute, our midfielder Neil Robinson had to leave the field after he was on the receiving end of a two-footed tackle, and his ankle ligament damage was so serious that he was unable to play professional football again. On top of that, in the 35th minute, Kevan Smith sustained a head wound that required several stitches. As he lay on the pitch receiving treatment from our physio, an old woman in the Northwich end shouted, 'I hope he's swallowed his tongue and he dies.' After ten minutes of treatment, Kevan returned to the fray with his head swathed in bandages. He required further attention later as his stitches burst open during the game and the wound had to be re-stitched.

In the 55th minute the hosts scored. Then, two minutes later our goalkeeper Mark Prudhoe and John Stringer both went for a 50-50 ball. Prudhoe, however, came out worse and received a nasty gash to his thigh from the opposing player's raking studs and had to be stretchered off. He was then taken to the local hospital where he was kept in overnight for observation. The tackle that caused this appalling injury was only punished with a booking, and yet it kept Prudhoe out of the side for more than five weeks. After this particular incident, Brian Little and his opposing number, Cliff Roberts, became embroiled in a heated argument, which one of the linesmen managed to bring under control, and the end result was that our forward John Borthwick went in goal. It was hardly a surprise that we lost this bruising encounter 1-0 and dropped to second in the table behind Barnet.

WELLING UNITED V DARLINGTON – 1989/90

The final match of the 1989/90 season, Welling United away in May 1990, would be a truly nailbiting affair as Darlington needed a victory in order to secure promotion back to the Football League at the first attempt.

We set off from Darlington early on Saturday morning. There were three of us in the car that day: Ian, a lad called Graham Dixon from Bishop Auckland, and me. When we arrived in London at about midday we dropped the car off outside Stephen Lowson's house in Bounds Green and then caught a southbound train across the Thames to Welling, where we met up in a pub with fellow Darlington fans Trevor Rutter, Brian Elsey and Phil Rutter.

Well over 1,000 Darlington fans packed into the away end of the leafy Park View Road ground that day.

There was a carnival mood among them and some supporters had entered into the spirit of the occasion by wearing fancy dress, such as a clown's outfit, while a veteran fan called Brian (now no longer with us) even turned up sporting his kilt.

To cap it all it, was a scorching day, with temperatures well into the 80s, the pitch was bone-hard and the away fans were exposed to the baking sun, since the ground largely consisted of open terracing.

But what an unforgettable experience it was! We got there early and the atmosphere was absolutely brilliant. The game wasn't a particularly good spectacle from a purist's point of view, but the meaning of it was more important than the action itself. With only three minutes remaining, Paul Emson was brought down by a clumsy late tackle on the left wing. Andy Toman cleverly swung in a cross to the far side of the penalty area where substitute Gary Coatsworth rose unchallenged to send a looping header past former Crystal Palace goalkeeper Paul Barron. It was his first ever senior goal.

I went wild as the whole of the away end erupted. Some people won't be able to understand that, but if your heart is in a club you kick every ball and save every shot, as if your life depended on it. Besides, the word 'fan' is just a shorter version of 'fanatic', which, as my dictionary says, is someone who is 'inspired by a god, frenzied, mad'.

I certainly behaved like a madman that day when we achieved promotion back to the Football League, having been relegated the previous season. Words couldn't explain my exhilaration when this was confirmed at the final whistle. 'We are back in the big time,' I thought as Ian pushed me out of the ground, more than an hour after the final whistle had been blown.

3

The 1990s

DARLINGTON V SWINDON TOWN –
LEAGUE CUP SECOND ROUND FIRST
LEG 1990/91

After a one-year absence, Darlington kicked off the 1990/91 season back in the Football League. Brian Little only made two signings during the summer – midfielder Mick Tait to his squad, on a free transfer from Reading, and youngster Michael Trotter from Middlesbrough. Other than those two, he kept faith with the players who had served him so well during the previous season.

The team started the new campaign with a 1-0 defeat at Gillingham, but then things improved with victories over Burnley and Halifax Town and draws against Walsall, York City and Wrexham, so after the opening month of the season, Darlington sat a handy eighth in the Fourth Division table with nine points from six games. Their return to the Football League meant that they were once again eligible to compete in the League Cup. In the first round they overcame Blackpool over two legs due to the away goals rule (0-0 at Feethams and 1-1 at Bloomfield Road after extra time) and the draw for the second round paired the Quakers with Swindon Town, again to be played over two legs. The first leg was at Feethams on Tuesday, 25 September and I attended with Ian.

At the time, the Robins should really have been a top-flight side. They had finished the previous season in fourth place in the Second Division (now the Championship) and had beaten Sunderland 1-0 in the play-off final at Wembley at the end of May to secure their place in the First Division. Ten days later, however, it became apparent that they had fallen foul of Football League rules and had been found guilty of making irregular payments to players and were relegated two divisions. They appealed that decision and had their punishment reduced to one relegation, so in effect, they remained in the Second Division and Sunderland were promoted to the top tier in their place.

Manager Ossie Ardiles managed to keep the majority of his squad together and they'd shaken off their disappointment to make a decent start to the new season. By the time they visited Feethams they sat fourth in the Second Division, with 13 points from seven games. They named an unchanged side after a 4-2 win at Oxford on the previous Saturday, remaining at full strength minus skipper Colin Calderwood who was out injured with ligament damage. His place in the side had been taken by Dave Bennett (brother of Gary, who later played for Darlington), a £50,000 signing from Sheffield Wednesday the previous week. Brian Little also named an unchanged 11 after a 1-1 draw at Wrexham. David Corner had received a knock during the game but had recovered to keep his place against Town. Their only absentee was central defender Jimmy Willis, who was still recovering after breaking his leg at Telford the previous April.

A crowd of 4,037 turned out at Feethams to see what promised to be an entertaining game between two strong, in-form sides. The visitors started brightly and completely dominated the first 20 minutes with their fluent, push and run, passing style. The Quakers were struggling to get into the game but still managed the two best chances of the half when hitting Town on the break. In the ninth minute Paul Emson fired in a close-range shot which was saved in spectacular fashion by Swindon's former Manchester United keeper Fraser Digby, and in the 23rd minute John Borthwick hit a fierce drive, but Digby proved his agility again with another flying save. Both chances were created by David Cork, who also had two goals disallowed, one for pushing and one for offside. At the other end, Mark Prudhoe made two good saves to keep Duncan Shearer out. The half finished goalless but ended on a sour note after a tackle from behind by

Darlington's midfielder Gary Gill left Dave Bennett with a broken left leg.

Darlington began the second half on top. Digby saved shots from Borthwick and Cork with his legs, before he was finally beaten in the 50th minute. Les McJannet slipped a neat ball to Gill down the right-hand edge of the box. He had timed his run perfectly to stay onside and his square ball across the face of the goal was met by Cork, who tucked it neatly under Digby from six yards out.

Swindon tried to hit back but Little's men always looked capable of more goals. Andy Toman was next to try his luck but lashed a fierce volley just wide and into the side netting in the 61st minute. Twelve minutes from time, the home side got the second goal that their play deserved. Borthwick broke from his own half, evading several tackles, before slipping the ball to Cork, who was upended by Ross Maclaren. Cork managed to force the ball into the net as he went down, but the referee had already awarded the penalty. Frank Gray made no mistake from the spot. Things got even better for Darlington in the 86th minute when John Gittens made a complete mess of an attempted headed back pass from a McJannet cross, leaving Cork with a simple close-range tap-in for his second of the night, to complete a resounding, if somewhat unexpected, 3-0 win.

Things went horribly wrong for Darlington in the second leg, played at the County Ground on 9 October, a game that I again attended with Ian.

Full-back McJannet missed the encounter with a hamstring injury and the Quakers' reshuffled defence just couldn't handle a rampant Swindon side, inspired by big-money new signing Micky Hazard. Town wiped out Darlington's advantage with three first-half goals and completed the tie with a 70th-minute winner to dump Darlington out 4-3 on aggregate. As the old saying goes, at least now Darlington could concentrate on the league.

MAIDSTONE UNITED V DARLINGTON – 1990/91

Perhaps the most memorable match of the 1990/91 season, for purely personal reasons rather than football ones, was at Maidstone United in October 1990.

By now the train journey from Darlington to King's Cross had become a well-trodden path to fixtures in the south of England and we knew all of its familiar landmarks by heart. However, Ian and I still managed to find plenty to talk about, aided no doubt by the fact that our tongues were constantly being lubricated by numerous cans of lager which we had bought from the buffet car. We also had a third travelling companion that day, Phil Rutter.

When we got to London we rendezvoused with Stephen, who had himself been drinking solidly all day. Later, we met up with Brian Elsey and Trevor Rutter in the Courthouse pub, which is about half a mile from Dartford train station.

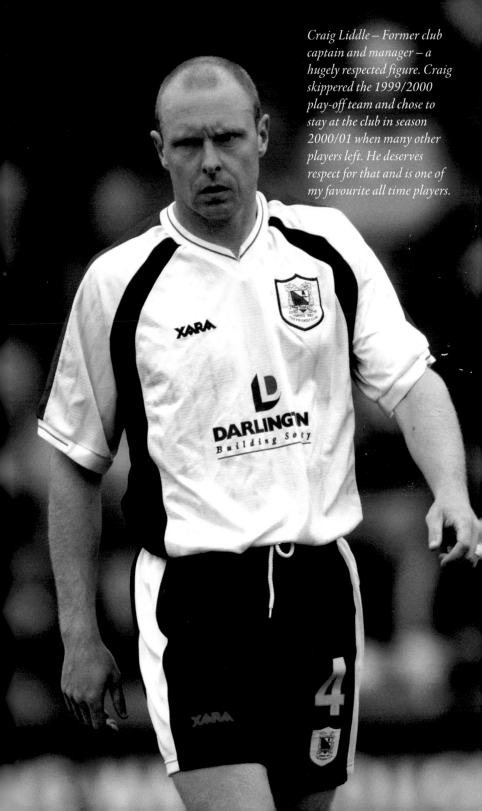

Craig Liddle – Former club captain and manager – a hugely respected figure. Craig skippered the 1999/2000 play-off team and chose to stay at the club in season 2000/01 when many other players left. He deserves respect for that and is one of my favourite all time players.

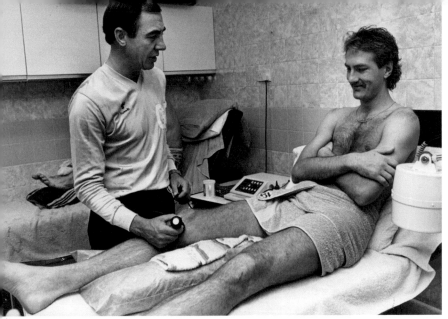

Kevan Smith – Receiving treatment for an injury following his move to First Division Coventry City in 1986. Kevan captained the club to three promotions: 1984/85, 1989/90 and 1990/91. Kevan is another of my all time favourite players.

David Speedie – Following his £65,000 move to Chelsea in 1982, David went on to represent Scotland and play for several First Division clubs including Liverpool, Coventry City and Blackburn Rovers.

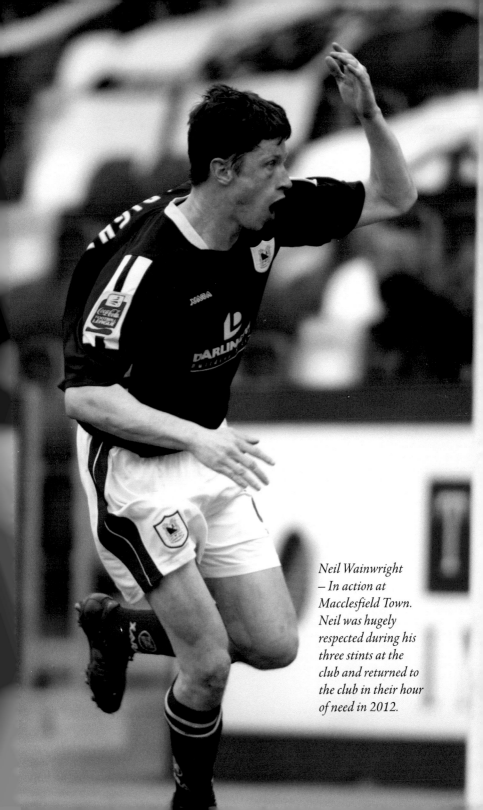

Neil Wainwright – In action at Macclesfield Town. Neil was hugely respected during his three stints at the club and returned to the club in their hour of need in 2012.

Marco Gabbiadini – Marco was Darlington's leading goalscorer in season 1999/2000, the season the Quakers narrowly missed out on promotion following their 1-0 defeat against Peterborough United in May 2000. He was hugely popular with the fans and scored many spectacular goals.

Mark Prudhoe – Goalkeeper Mark won two promotions with the club in seasons 1989/90 and 1990/91 and is one of the best goalkeepers to represent the club in my lifetime. The guy is a legend!

Alan Walsh – following his £18,000 move to Bristol City in 1984. Alan is the club's joint record goalscorer with exactly 100 goals and was signed from Middlesbrough in October 1978.

Gary Brown – in action in a pre-season friendly against Sunderland. Gary joined the club in 2012 following their relegation to the Northern League, and apart from a brief stint at Shildon, he mostly skippered to club to three promotions in seasons 2012/13, 2014/15 and 2015/16. Gary is one of my favourite post-2012 players.

Stephen Thompson in action in the FA Cup first round tie against Walsall in season 2019/2020. Stephen is the club's other joint record goalscorer with 100 goals and currently plays for Stockton Town.

Will Hatfield – in action in the FA Cup first round tie against Walsall in season 2019/2020. Will joined the club from Guiseley in 2015. He was a committed midfielder until his departure in 2022 when he joined AFC Fylde. Will was one of the best midfielders to represent the club in the post-2012 era.

Maidstone had sold their London Road ground to the MFI furniture group in 1988. Since their promotion from the Vauxhall Conference in 1989, taking relegated Darlington's place in the Football League, they had been sharing Southern League Dartford's Watling Street ground while they were engaged in a planning dispute with the local council over a proposal to build a new stadium.

Once inside the ground, I ended up being perched rather precariously on the terraces and so I said to Phil, 'Move me along a bit, mate, I can't see a bloody thing.' But rather than shove me sideways, he pushed me forwards and I fell headlong down the steps and was knocked out cold.

The next thing I remember was being put in an ambulance, though I must have had some of my wits about me because I apparently insisted on buying a match programme before I left for the hospital and wouldn't budge until I got one!

Once at the hospital, despite suffering from a severe headache, my concussion had eased somewhat and I wanted to get back to the game. I explained to the nurse that I'd forked out £40 for the train fare and wasn't prepared to miss the rest of the game, so would she stitch my head wound because I wanted to leave. The nurse, however, had other ideas and said I ought to stay in the hospital overnight as a precaution, to which I replied, 'I don't think so!' so she quickly stitched up my cut and we hurriedly left.

Outside the hospital, we hailed a cab and extravagantly offered the driver £15 if he could get us back to the ground within five minutes. He drove like a bat out of hell and I saw the last two goals that sealed our victory, so the extra expense was worth it in the end.

We won 3-2 with goals from David Cork, John Borthwick and Andy Toman. Unfortunately, all I can remember about the match is the last two goals, which is a shame as, according to the lads, Darlo played some of their best football of the season that day.

After the game, we went to London's West End to celebrate our victory. However, things were still very hazy for me – I didn't feel very well at all and had a stinking headache, several stitches in my wound and a massive bandage wrapped around my head.

To be on the safe side, one of the lads phoned up my mother to explain what had happened to me, and she told him not to let me fall asleep or get drunk. Fatal. Stupidly, I downed seven pints and fell asleep in the pub! So much for motherly advice. It didn't do me any harm as I felt fine the following day and travelled back to Darlington without any problems at all.

DARLINGTON V CARDIFF CITY – 1990/91

On New Year's Day 1991, Darlington fans were hoping that the coming 12 months would be as exciting and as successful as the previous year had been. Brian Little was spearheading the Quakers on another promotion hunt in the Fourth Division. As the year dawned, Darlington sat fourth in the table on 34 points, with nine wins and seven draws from their 20 games played.

Their opponents on the first day of the year were Cardiff City (again I went to this game with Ian) who would be making only their third appearance at Feethams for a league game. They'd visited twice in the 1980s, suffering a 4-1 defeat in a Third Division game in October 1985 and then escaping with a goalless draw in February 1988 in a drab Third Division encounter. The Bluebirds had warmed up for their trip to Feethams with two home victories over the festive period, 3-1 against Carlisle on Boxing Day and then 1-0 against Halifax three days later. The two wins moved City up into mid-table, where they now sat only five points behind Darlo and were hopeful that 1991 would see them push up the table towards the promotion places.

Darlington's long trip to Aldershot on Boxing Day had been postponed due to a waterlogged pitch (Ian and I actually arrived at the ground, only to find out that the game had been called off) so their only festive outing was a 1-1 draw at Scarborough on 29 December. Drew Coverdale had scored after only 31 seconds, but they had to settle for a point when the same player handled in the box and Boro equalised from the spot.

Little kept the same starting 11 but made changes on the bench. Lee Ellison and Gary Coatsworth were both injured and unavailable, but Phil Linacre and David

Corner were both back in contention after recovering from injuries of their own. Also available again was winger Steve Mardenborough, who had missed the Scarborough game after injuring himself getting off the coach after the wasted trip to Aldershot.

A holiday crowd of 3,151 braved the absolutely atrocious weather to watch the game. Strong winds and heavy rain made for difficult playing conditions but the home side revelled in the Feethams mud, making light of the sticky pitch and starting the game with some enterprising football. They opened the scoring in the 14th minute when David Cork held the ball up well on the edge of the box before rolling it into the path of the onrushing Les McJannet. He ran on a couple of strides into the penalty area and then thumped a low drive beyond Roger Hansbury's despairing dive. Cardiff hit back and Cohen Griffith hit a low shot that skidded off the wet turf, but Mark Prudhoe went full-length to keep it out.

It was to be Prudhoe's only anxious moment of the half as the home side took complete control. Cork made it 2-0 in the 37th minute with a superb finish. Exchanging passes with fellow striker John Borthwick down the left, he found himself on the corner of the penalty area and cleverly chipped the ball across Hansbury into the far top corner of the net. It was 3-0 six minutes later as Prudhoe used the following wind to launch a prodigious goal kick deep into the City half, where it was misjudged by the visiting defenders and allowed to bounce into the penalty area, Jimmy Willis sticking out a long leg to loop the ball over the stranded keeper.

Little's men, three goals to the good and with the game already won, left the pitch at half-time to a rousing ovation. They could and indeed should have made it four early in the second half when Cork and man-of-the-match Borthwick both had close-range shots kicked off the line. Play briefly switched to the other end where Mark Taylor thought he'd pulled a goal back, but his shot was brilliantly steered around the post by Andy Toman with Prudhoe well beaten.

Darlington continued to hold the upper hand, despite playing into the wind and rain, and Gary Gill went close with a shot when a square ball to Cork may have been the better option. The home side scored the fourth goal that their play deserved in the 64th minute after a foul on Toman. Coverdale's inch-perfect free kick was met by a thumping Willis header. Hansbury did well to keep that out but could only watch as Mick Tait hit the rebound into the empty net. Cardiff scored a consolation goal three minutes from time when Griffith, their best player on the day, turned home a left-wing cross from close range to deny the impressive Prudhoe a clean sheet.

The 4-1 win lifted Darlo to third in the table, and another solid home victory, 3-1 against Carlisle four days later, took them to the top of the league.

NORTHAMPTON TOWN V DARLINGTON
– 1990/91

In April 1991, Ian and I went on the train to Northampton. We then changed at Peterborough where we met Stephen. The three of us then caught another train to our final destination, arriving just after opening time. We went round a few pubs including the Penny Whistle, the Racecourse, and several others, the names of which are lost in time.

Once inside the ground the three of us managed to gain admittance into the away end without any problems. In fact, we were afforded what can only be described as an excellent view of a pulsating Darlington performance.

Darlo scored early and were 3-0 up by half-time through goals from John Borthwick, David Cork and Michael Trotter.

They were in cruise control for the whole of the second half and simply saw the game out with a thoroughly professional performance.

This was the Quakers' best display of the season, especially as the Cobblers were near the top of the table. As we left the ground, the three of us agreed that, if they played like that for the rest of the season, Darlo would win promotion easily.

After the match, we stayed in Northampton for a few beers and then caught the train to Peterborough. Prior to leaving, we had a few drinks in the Station Hotel, before polishing off several more cans on the train. By the time we arrived at Darlington station, Ian was so drunk that I don't know how he managed to get me safely down on to the platform. Nevertheless, looking back, it was one of our best away trips of the season.

DARLINGTON V ROCHDALE – 1990/91

In May 1991 Darlo played Rochdale at Feethams in their final league match of the season, which Darlo had to win to ensure promotion to the old Third Division. As per usual, I went with Ian. The pair of us sat in the East Stand paddock.

As early as the third minute, we witnessed David Cork hit the bar after a brilliant run and cross from Mitch Cook. The same player made amends in the ninth minute when John Borthwick flicked on a long goal kick from Mark Prudhoe, Cork chesting it down and sliding the ball home past visiting keeper Keith Welch to send the 9,160 crowd into raptures. The Quakers continued to control the match without managing to increase their lead, but the second half was only a minute old when Jimmy Willis was tripped in the box and the referee had no hesitation in pointing to the spot. Frank Gray sealed a 2-0 victory with a sweetly struck penalty – his eighth goal of a memorable season. As full time approached, the referee saw the encroaching fans behind him and sensibly blew his whistle.

After the match, Ian and I went to Darlington Cricket Club where the players and the fans were celebrating promotion. I can recall that each of the players stood on a chair in the middle of the room and did a turn for the fans. When David Cork took the floor, he put his finger to his lips, told everybody to be quiet, and then sang, 'We Are the Champions'. For the second season in a row, we really were the champions. I have to say, it was like being in a dream.

Later that evening, Ian, Trevor, Phil, a lad called Neil Parkinson and I caught a train to Bishop Auckland where Graham (the guy who'd taken us to Welling the previous season) was to hold a celebratory party. He had a full-sized snooker table in his house and Ian tried to teach me how to play the game, with predictably disastrous results. We stayed there overnight, drinking beer and eating pizzas, and came back on the Sunday morning with massive hangovers.

AFC BOURNEMOUTH V DARLINGTON – 1991/92

An away trip to Bournemouth was our first match of the 1991/92 season and I went there on the supporters' club coach with Ian. Darlington had clinched their second promotion in two seasons to take their place in the Third Division.

Unfortunately, manager Brian Little left that summer to take over at Leicester City. He was replaced by his assistant Frank Gray, who turned down the chance to become Little's number two and remained at Feethams.

Ian and I left at five o'clock in the morning and we were there for around 12.30pm with one stop en route at Tamworth services. I remember that the two of us had our breakfast there, all washed down with a pot of tea. Unfortunately, to our horror, we noticed cigarette ash floating in our cups after Ian had poured the tea! He therefore took the teapot back to the counter. Given that we didn't have time to drink the replacement, as the coach was about to leave, we decided to tip the remains of our meal into it in order that they couldn't recycle the contents. Childish? Certainly. However, it made me smile as we watched the woman who was clearing our table shake her head in our direction as we left.

Once in Bournemouth we went to a pub, the name of which escapes me, where there were quite a few Darlo fans already in there. One of them was drunkenly trying to play the piano and the lads with him were attempting to sing along, which was actually quite funny to watch. It reminded me of a very poor karaoke act.

Leaving the drunken pianist and his cohorts behind, we had a few more drinks in Bournemouth's supporters' club, after which we proceeded to the match. I watched from the disabled area with Ian. Since the area was on a slope, a steward put some wooden blocks under my wheels to stop my wheelchair from shooting down the incline. They certainly did the trick.

Darlo started off the way they had finished the previous season and won the game 2-1 with Jimmy Willis scoring the winner after Alex Watson, Bournemouth's former Liverpool defender, had put through his own goal.

Nevertheless, we were the better of the two teams and thoroughly deserved our narrow victory.

EXETER CITY V DARLINGTON – 1991/92

In October 1991 I went on one of my least favourite away trips – to Exeter City – in the company of John Gray.

Once inside the ground, we were met by a cocky steward who asked us to move from the sparsely populated away end to the disabled area. I therefore asked him, 'Do you mind if I finish my drink first and then I'll gladly move?' I had a cup of hot Bovril in one hand and a pie in the other and it was ten minutes before kick-off. John then chipped in with, 'Come on, mate, be reasonable, there are only 20 people in the away end.' The steward, however, was unmoved and said, 'Any more lip from you and you'll be chucked out.' With that, he made John move me straight away, which meant that I had to sit among the home fans and became separated from John.

As a disabled football fan, this certainly wasn't the first example of discrimination and shabby treatment that I'd encountered on my travels. It's something that you get used to when you are a wheelchair user. The steward acted totally unreasonably where common sense could and should have prevailed. It's not surprising that some of my friends don't like pushing my wheelchair at matches – you can hardly blame them. The steward's attitude seemed all the more silly to me since the away end was virtually empty. You could have understood his point of view if that section of the ground had been full. It seemed to me that his whole attitude was a case of bureaucracy gone mad. Consequently, I ended up being put in the disabled area among the home fans where some idiots who were standing behind the disabled area thought it would be fun to spit at me. I told a different steward about it, but nothing was done, as he seemed more interested in watching the match.

To add insult to injury, I was overcharged by £2. The home fans paid £5 whereas I was charged £7 and that was against the Football League rules. So, afterwards, I wrote a letter of complaint to the Exeter manager, Alan Ball, but the club saw nothing wrong with my treatment.

Later, I also wrote to the Football League at Lytham St Annes and they upheld my complaint. Exeter offered me my £2 back; I refused as that wasn't the real basis of my complaint. They shouldn't have behaved in the manner they did. The £2 was neither here nor there.

Anyway, back to the game in question. To complete a miserable day, we lost 4-1, Steve Moran, the former Southampton and Leicester City star, scoring all four of Exeter's goals with youngster Lee Ellison scoring our consolation from the penalty spot. To make matters worse, Jimmy Willis was sent off for the Quakers in the 77th minute for repeatedly fouling Moran. This completed what was an unhappy, but at the same time memorable, day out.

DARLINGTON V HARTLEPOOL UNITED – 1991/92

The old enemy, Hartlepool United, visited Feethams on 2 November. In an attempt to curb the two sets of supporters from excessive pre-match drinking, the police asked for the kick-off to be brought forward. Ian and I were therefore two of the first customers in the Pennyweight pub in Darlington's market square for opening time.

After a couple of quick pints, we headed for the ground – I went in the East Stand paddock with Ian opting for a more traditional vantage point in the Tin Shed.

It couldn't have been a more one-sided derby. Two goals from Lee Ellison, a John MacPhail own goal and a fourth from on-loan Celtic forward Dugald McCarrison gave the Quakers a morale-boosting 4-0 victory.

Interestingly, a few weeks previously I had interviewed McCarrison for the *Darlington Advertiser* (a second job that I had for a while) and I remember that when winger Steve Mardenborough had gone to fetch him from the dressing room, the Scottish player had thought it was a wind-up because I was a wheelchair user. But eventually I managed to persuade him that I was genuine and he gave me the interview, which was later published.

DARLINGTON V TORQUAY UNITED – 1992/93

The 1992/93 season kicked off with Billy McEwan (now no longer with us) in the manager's seat at Feethams. The previous four seasons had been eventful to say the least. Relegation from the Football League, followed by back-to-back Conference and Fourth Division championships, followed immediately by relegation back to where the club had started. And 1992/93 was also the first season of the Premier League, with all divisions subsequently being renamed, so although the Quakers had been relegated from the Third Division at the end of the previous season, they found themselves at the lower tier but still playing Third Division football.

McEwan had been appointed in the summer after seeing off competition from John Bird, Viv Busby, David McCreery, Kevan Smith and Ray Hankin for the job. Hankin had been in temporary charge since the sacking of Frank Gray in the previous February. McEwan had formerly managed Rotherham and Sheffield United and came with a reputation as a strict disciplinarian.

The team made a mixed start to the new season with two wins and two defeats in the first five games but then three defeats on the trot had dropped Darlington to the bottom of the league table with seven points from eight games. Teams level on points were separated by goals scored, rather than goal difference at that time. Five teams had seven points, but Darlo had only scored seven goals, the lowest total in the league.

The fixture at home to Torquay United (I watched from the East Stand paddock with Ian) would take place on Friday, 2 October. The Quakers had switched some of their early home games to Friday nights as an experiment to try and increase attendances, the idea being not to clash with Middlesbrough's home games in the Premier League.

McEwan had selection problems for the game. Skipper Kevan Smith (calf), Mark Sunley (ankle), Anthony Isaacs (flu) and Gary Hinchley (knee) all missed out. There were also doubts about keeper Mark Prudhoe with an injured hip, Steve Mardenborough with a knee injury and Ian Juryeff with a back strain, but the three were deemed fit enough to play. Steve Tupling had been signed on a short-term contract to provide cover for Hinchley and Sunley and he was expected to play at full-back against one of his former clubs. Striker Mark Dobie had also previously played for Torquay United and would be looking to get one over on his former employers. The visitors included Justin Fashanu in their line-up, the much-travelled striker having been appointed as assistant manager during the summer.

The switch to Friday nights didn't seem to work as only 1,423 hardy fans turned out at a rain-soaked Feethams to see the game. They saw Darlo make a bright start and with better luck could have had two goals in the opening five minutes. Firstly Steve Mardenborough crashed a header into the side netting from a Nick Pickering free kick, then moments later Mark Dobie's cross from the left was met by a flying Ian Juryeff header, but visiting keeper Matthew Lowe reacted well to save. Torquay always looked dangerous on the break and Scott Colcombe went close but his goalbound shot was brilliantly blocked by a brave Mardenborough challenge. Then Fashanu was unlucky with a powerful header that went straight into Mark Prudhoe's arms. The home side were well on top though and Mardenborough brought another good save out of Lowe, then Mark Dobie curled a shot just wide.

The opening goal of the game came in the 28th minute and was scored completely against the run of play as the visitors took the lead. Sean Joyce received a throw-in from Paul Hall and rifled in a low shot from the edge of the area that skidded off the wet surface past the helpless Prudhoe.

The Quakers' confidence visibly drained and it wasn't until the second half that they posed any real threat again, and they equalised from the penalty spot in the 53rd minute. Steve Gaughan sent Mardenborough away down the right and his cross fell to Dobie, whose shot was blocked. In the ensuing goalmouth scramble, Juryeff was upended by Matt Gardiner. Dobie calmly sent Lowe the wrong way from the spot to record his first Darlington goal.

Confidence came flooding back and 15 minutes later, the home side were in front, Tim Parkin netting his first for the club with a header from a Pickering free kick. The Quakers were now well on top and Mardenborough, O'Shaughnessy and Dobson all went close before Mardenborough made it 3-1 in the 80th minute. Gaughan and Juryeff combined on the halfway line to send the speedy winger racing clear down the right to score with a powerful low shot, fired under the advancing keeper. There was still time for substitute Andy Toman to add a fourth goal, collecting the ball 25 yards out and picking his way through a crowded area to score a brilliant solo goal.

Incredibly, once the Saturday's results were taken into account, the 4-1 win lifted Darlington eight places in the table, up to 14th. They spent the rest of the season hovering just below mid-table, never really in danger at the bottom, but also never really threatening to break into the top half and towards the play-off places. They finished the season in 15th place with 50 points from their 42 games. The Torquay match was the last of three to be switched to a Friday night, as the anticipated increase in attendances never materialised. This probably had very little to do with a clash with Middlesbrough and a lot to do with Darlington's poor home form. They suffered ten defeats in 21 games at Feethams and only gained 21 points at home, compared to 29 won away.

DONCASTER ROVERS V DARLINGTON – 1993/94

As poor starts to the season go, 1993/94 takes some beating – no wins in the first 13 league games and only seven goals scored is not exactly promotion form! Also included in that dismal run was an 11-1 aggregate hammering at the hands of Bradford City in the first round of the League Cup.

Something clearly had to change, and the hugely unpopular manager Billy McEwan paid the price. Officially he resigned, but whether he jumped just before he was about to be pushed is a matter of conjecture. Former Hartlepool United boss Alan Murray was given the task of reviving Darlington's fortunes, and he immediately installed Eddie Kyle as his assistant. Their first game in charge was away at Scunthorpe United and resulted in a 3-0 defeat. Their first home game was on the following Tuesday evening against Colchester, and no one could have predicted how that would turn out.

Darlington doubled their season's goal tally in one action-packed evening as they thumped Colchester 7-3 in front of 1,299 fans, all of them hoping that Murray could lead them up the table. I can remember that former Newcastle United winger Peter Kirkham was in great form for Darlo that night. The Quakers managed to win their next two home games as well, but as the Christmas fixtures approached, things still looked bleak with Darlo second-bottom in the Third Division table with

15 points from 19 games. The only team behind them were Northampton Town, who occupied the solitary relegation spot.

The first game of the festive programme saw the Quakers beaten 3-1 at home by Carlisle United, in front of a season's best crowd of 4,831. The following afternoon, Tuesday, 28 December, they would travel to Belle Vue to take on Doncaster Rovers. I went to this match with Ian in his car. Rovers were having a mixed season; only a month previously they'd been sat in sixth place and were eyeing a promotion charge, but three defeats on the trot had dropped them into the bottom half of the table. They sat in 14th place with 26 points from their 19 games. Murray made one change to his starting 11, Mark Sunley replacing former Manchester United player Lawrie Pearson. Sunley would play at right-back in a five-man defence with skipper Steve O'Shaughnessy dropping back from midfield to play alongside Matty Appleby and Andy Crosby in the centre of defence.

Doncaster appealed for volunteers on the morning of the game and supporters of both clubs joined together to clear snow off the pitch to allow the match to go ahead. A crowd of 2,194 turned out and saw the visitors take the lead in the tenth minute with virtually their first attack. Mark Sunley swung in a free kick which was touched on by Paul Cross and volleyed home by Gary Chapman at the far post.

The Quakers very nearly increased their lead in the opening minute of the second half but Lee Ellison's close-range effort was beaten away by Donny keeper Andy Beasley. The home side then got well on top and grabbed a deserved equaliser in the 58th minute when a Danny Williamson cross was headed home by Don Page. Rovers' momentum was interrupted two minutes later though by a floodlight failure. Only one light was left on in the whole of the ground – and that was in the press box.

The players left the field for seven minutes while the problem was fixed, and Darlo used the break to regroup and sort themselves out. They took control after the restart and regained the lead in the 68th minute. Steve Gaughan, playing against his former club, made a good run to the edge of the box before squaring the ball to Ellison, who fired home. Things got even better for Darlington eight minutes later when Ellison controlled a long clearance from goalkeeper Darren Collier and flicked the ball into the path of Robbie Painter, who beat Beasley with a right-footed shot. Darlo had to reorganise two minutes later when Collier was flattened by home centre-forward Kevin Hulme and had to leave the field for stitches to a nose wound. His place was taken by 17-year-old debutant Ryan Scott, who made his one and only appearance for the club.

The enforced switch didn't affect them too much and they almost added a fourth as Painter fired wide from six yards out, and then the striker was unlucky not to score deep in injury time when his drive from Chapman's pass was headed off the line by a Doncaster defender.

The 3-1 victory was Darlington's first three points of the season on the road, and it was their third victory in succession at Belle Vue, which had become a happy hunting ground after 1-0 wins on their two previous visits.

The result lifted Murray's men to third from bottom but only two wins in the next ten ensured that they never escaped the battle to avoid bottom spot. They spent much of the season in last place and with four games left they found themselves three points adrift of Northampton, but a late rally saw them win three out of the last four to leapfrog the Cobblers into 21st place. Northampton escaped relegation to the Conference because Kidderminster's ground wasn't up to standard and they were denied promotion to the Football League.

HARTLEPOOL UNITED V DARLINGTON – 1995/96

In September 1995 I was involved in a sponsored wheelchair push to Hartlepool, which I will now recount.

The words 'disability' and 'charity' very often seem to exist side by side like 'fish' and 'chips'. Ideally, state support for people who happen to be born with a disability should be sufficient to make charitable handouts unnecessary, but in practice it isn't, which means getting involved yourself and making things happen. I must admit that I'm very much against charity on a personal level – I

certainly don't consider myself to be a charity case –
but on this particular occasion I was actually helping
someone else who was less fortunate than me.

When Ian and I embarked on the journey from the
Colburn Lodge pub to Hartlepool, a distance of some
40-odd miles, we were spurred on by the plight of a little
girl called Sharah-Lea Minshull, who lived in Catterick
and had been disabled since birth with cerebral palsy.

We planned to give half the money that we raised
to her appeal, since she needed some special equipment
in order to help her speak. The rest of the money was to
be donated to the special baby care unit at Darlington
Memorial Hospital, which was where Ian's twin girls,
Victoria and Leanne, had been cared for after they were
born prematurely.

Given our starting point of Catterick Garrison, Ian
and I planned the expedition to Hartlepool like a military
operation and received numerous sponsorship pledges.
John Gray drove one of the backup cars and Ian's brother-
in-law Darren drove the other, which contained my spare
wheelchair, to be used in case anything happened to my
everyday one.

On the evening of the walk, we set off from the pub
at midnight, and it was absolutely bucketing with rain.
Despite the dreadful weather we still made good time.

Unfortunately, during the journey, John's electrics
kept cutting out as a result of driving at only four miles
per hour for long periods of time. As it was necessary for

one of the backup cars to stay with us throughout the trip, it being a criminal offence to do a charity walk without one in attendance, we had a problem. It was obvious that neither of the two cars would make it because the rain was badly affecting their electrics. John's car in particular, a Honda Civic, was quite old and it was constantly grinding to a halt. So, after much discussion, Ian and I decided that one car would stay with us for a mile or so while the other went on ahead. Then when the first car drew level with the second the roles were reversed. So, with each car taking turns to accompany the pair of us, this made things much easier for both us and, more importantly, for the drivers.

That night the two of us talked about football and anything else that happened to enter our minds while he was pushing me along. We did, however, encounter one problem with the wheelchair we were using when the wheel buckled, but that was easily remedied; we simply swapped it for the spare wheelchair.

I remember we both wore some waterproofs which Ian had borrowed from the army base where he worked, but they certainly didn't live up to their name. I was absolutely soaked to the skin due to the heavy, incessant rain. I have to admit that I have never been so drenched in all my life as I was during that push – even my underpants were wringing wet.

We stopped off en route at a pub in the Hartlepool area called the Owton Lodge, near Billingham – Ian knew the landlord well as previously he had worked as a part-time barman in the Colburn Lodge. In fact, both pubs were owned by the same brewery at the time. We both got changed and put on some dry clothes. After I had been changed, I drank a couple of pints and ate a few sandwiches before setting off again on the final leg of our journey.

John left us for the final stretch, because he had promised to meet some friends, so from then on we operated with only one backup car. But this didn't present a problem because by then it was daylight.

We arrived at Victoria Park at about 11 o'clock and went to their supporters' club for a few pints. Purely to avoid the risk of dehydration, you understand! I was shattered by then and could hardly stay awake. Despite this, after obtaining permission from a Hartlepool United official to collect some more money at the main entrance, we raised a further £300, which was absolutely brilliant.

Though we had both completed the same wheelchair push before, we beat our previous time, and I felt proud of our achievement because it was something that nobody could take away from us.

A few weeks later, after all the money had been collected, we organised a band night at the Colburn Lodge, and Stephen Lowson's former brother-in-law, who is the lead singer of a rockabilly group called The Skip Rats, played a gig to raise further funds. We ended up raising £1,000 in total and gave £500 each to Sharah-Lea and Darlington Memorial Hospital. I bottled out of handing the money over in person and got Kevan Smith, who kindly came along, to do it in my place. Former Darlington player Steve Tupling also came that night, along with manager Jim Platt and a few of the other squad members.

I have to say that without the invaluable assistance of John, Ian's family as a whole and especially Darren, we would never have accomplished the walk and raised so much money.

I honestly think that too many people are on the take these days and don't think about others. So, with this in mind, it was nice to be able to give something back for a change and seeing on the faces of those people at the presentation the pleasure we had given them made it all worthwhile.

And the result of the match, I hear you ask? Well, on that particular occasion our local derby was a secondary consideration.

I do recall that Mark Barnard was stretchered off after a clash of heads with Tony Canham in the first half.

Really, I have to admit that I was half-asleep for most of the game, but I do recall that it was a 1-1 draw with Pool scoring first through Keith Houchen in the 72nd minute and our goal coming from Anthony Carss in the 84th.

DONCASTER ROVERS V DARLINGTON – 1995/96

I knew that Ian wanted to go to Doncaster in March 1996. Unfortunately Lynne, his wife – now no longer – wasn't keen on him going. I therefore devised a plan that would enable him to accompany me. I rang her and promised her that we'd be back at 6.30pm at the latest. I knew we wouldn't be – Lynne said that as long as he was back by then and more importantly he had to remain sober she'd be happy for him to go. Ian couldn't believe his luck! I said that it must have been my charm that softened her attitude; it didn't really matter though – we were heading for Doncaster together.

On the day of the match, we caught a train at about ten in the morning, arriving in Doncaster at around 11 o'clock. We each consumed four cans of lager in 60 minutes. This proved to be the prelude for the day.

Our first stop on disembarking from the train was the bar in the station where we bumped into four other Darlo fans who had travelled up from London. However, although I know several fans from that area, as does Ian, neither of us recognised any of them. Nevertheless, this didn't stop us from accompanying them to a pub called The Railway, which is about five minutes' walk from the station. Our newfound friends said they were from south London – apparently they had decided to go to the game on the spur of the moment. One was called John; unfortunately, the names of the others are lost forever in the passage of time, though more likely the amount I drank that day also added to my amnesia. John certainly liked playing fruit machines; one of the regulars almost fell off his stool when he asked the barman to change a £20 note and then proceeded to feed the whole lot into the slot. Not surprisingly, he didn't win a penny.

On speaking to the Londoners, they seemed surprised that someone in a wheelchair would go to away matches. I said that in my opinion the wheelchair didn't matter as even if I'd been able-bodied I would have still gone to the games. John then went on to say that he 'admired' Ian for taking me to see Darlo play. Taking the words out of my mouth, Ian replied that my being in a wheelchair didn't make any difference to him. I got the impression that John wouldn't have the patience to accompany a wheelchair user to a match. This didn't in my opinion make him a bad person – just slightly ignorant.

The Railway was a small pub with several regulars who looked as though they had been in there most of their lives – in other word 'a man's pub'. They were pleasant enough though.

After drinking several pints, the six of us headed for the ground; we had to catch two cabs from the station as there were too many of us to fit in one. Ian struggled to put me in the car as we were rather the worse for wear, but as per usual he managed, eventually.

On arrival at Belle Vue we were separated from our London friends and I have never seen them again to this day.

Once inside the ground, the pair of us witnessed an excellent Darlo performance, with Robbie Blake particularly outstanding. From the outside looking in, Darlo fans got the feeling that co-manager David Hodgson didn't rate him, since earlier that season he had been sent out on loan to Waterford, a team in Ireland, and he looked at that time to be on his way out of the club. Things changed when David resigned in December 1995 (apparently, according to David, he and Jim Platt were both supposed to quit but Platt changed his mind and stayed) at half-time during the FA Cup tie against Rochdale. If Darlington had won that game, they would have played Liverpool.

At the time, the Quakers had a really good goalkeeper in Mike Pollitt, who the club wanted to sell to Notts County for £100,000. David wanted to keep him until after the Rochdale match. However, the club sold him beforehand, without the backing of the management duo. Hodgson stuck to his word and left. Platt staying on and taking over as manager could, looking from the outside in, have been considered as being disloyal. However, during one of our many conversations, David said they made up many years ago. This was good to hear. Getting back to Robbie Blake, he flourished after that and became a really important part of the team.

Anyway, returning to the game in question, Darlo ran Rovers ragged for most of the 90 minutes and eventually won 2-1 with goals from Gary Bannister and Blake. I can remember thinking that Doncaster looked a poor side; this was reflected by the fact that in 1995/96 they won only eight league games at home. That didn't matter to Ian and I; all we were interested in was obtaining the three points that kept us in contention for the play-offs.

After the match, the two of us headed back to The Railway. Ian mentioned that we really should head home after a pint. That was quickly forgotten when we started chatting to some of the regulars, most of whom had been there since Ian, the Londoners and I had first entered the pub that morning.

Anyway, at half past seven Ian rang Lynne; she lost her temper with him saying that he was supposed to be home by then. He said that he'd 'forgotten' about the time. Looking back, I don't suppose his slurred words helped to convince her of his sincerity! Ian's response was, 'In for a penny, in for a pound.' With those words of wisdom, he just carried on drinking.

While Ian was talking to Lynne, I got chatting to an elderly gentleman who was present at Doncaster's 10-0 annihilation of Darlington in 1963/64. He then took great delight in telling me about each of the goals. I have the programme from that particular game. When I mentioned this to him he instantly said that he'd give me

£50 for it. I politely declined his offer as I would never sell any of my programme collection. He seemed genuinely disappointed by my response.

On his return, Ian said that we'd catch the eight o'clock train. The old man I'd been talking to said that the clock near the bar was slow and it was already ten past eight! Much to my amusement, Ian's face went a deathly white in colour. He quickly realised that he would have to telephone Lynne again but asked me to do it on his behalf. I rang and said that I only had ten pence in change. When I explained about the clock she said that I must be more drunk than Ian to expect her to believe a story like that. Fortunately for me, the pips started to sound, and the phone went dead. Ian by now was in deep trouble. I said that we might as well have another pint, as there was nothing we could do and the next train wasn't until quarter past nine.

At nine o'clock we bid our farewells to our drinking partners and headed for the station. We were both rather the worse for wear after consuming more than ten pints during the day. The walk took ten minutes rather than the usual five, meaning that we only just made the train by the skin of our teeth.

Ian hardly said a word during our journey home. I tried to be positive and said at least Darlo had won the game and he had been there to see it, together with the fact that arguments always do have a tendency to blow over. I think that made him feel slightly better.

On our arrival back in Darlington we hailed a cab from the station rank. I was dropped off first and then Ian went home to face the music.

The day after the match Ian rang me and said that Lynne had gone crazy with him. The funny thing was that while she was shouting at him, all he could remember were my words, 'Darlo won and you were there to see it.'

SCUNTHORPE UNITED V DARLINGTON – 1995/96

I accompanied Ian to the final match of the 1995/96 season, at Scunthorpe United. This was a game that the Quakers simply had to win to have a chance of clinching automatic promotion. Memories of a previous visit were still fresh in my mind on the morning of the game – the 5-1 defeat on 6 May 1989 that consigned us to the Conference. Scunthorpe never did seem to be a happy hunting ground for Darlo. Even the manager, Mick Buxton, was the same as last time – now in his second spell at the club.

Ian picked me up in his car from my flat, the only other passenger to join us that day being his brother Graeme.

We left quite early at about 11 in the morning and soon found ourselves in the midst of a convoy of cars, making the same journey as ourselves. The *Northern Echo* later spoke of 2,000 Darlington fans travelling to Humberside.

When we arrived in Scunthorpe at around one o'clock, we parked the car near the Berkeley pub and saw the fans from both clubs sitting outside in the bright sunshine. After a few pints the three of us made our way to Glanford Park.

Ian managed to get me into the away end without any problems where we bumped into Stephen at half-time when the score was 2-0 to the Iron with goals from John Eyre in the fourth and 35th minutes.

Matty Appleby then converted a penalty in the 61st minute which sparked off a mass brawl among the home fans that spilled on to the pitch. After Anthony Carss's looping header found the net in the 68th minute, there was yet another pitch invasion, this time from the Darlington fans. Then Andy McFarlane scored for the Iron in the 87th minute only for Mark Barnard to equalise a minute later.

The nearest we came to getting the winner that we desperately needed was when a shot from Robbie Blake smacked against the bar in the dying seconds.

We were kept back inside the ground for a good ten minutes, so that the home fans could disperse. We waited anxiously for the score from Gigg Lane, because the match there had kicked off late. When we heard that Bury, who we were battling against for the last promotion place, had won, the disappointment was tangible. Automatic promotion had eluded us and we were now at the mercy of the play-offs.

Jim Platt would have to galvanise his team in order to achieve their goal of gaining promotion.

PLYMOUTH ARGYLE V DARLINGTON – PLAY-OFF FINAL AT WEMBLEY 1995/96

I'd only been to Wembley twice previously. The first time I had gone with Gavin to see England beat Hungary 1-0 in November 1981, and the second time was for the Sherpa Van Trophy Final between Wolves and Burnley alongside Ian and Stephen in May 1988, when Wolves won 2-0. I vowed then that I would never go back unless it was to see Darlington play. Well, little did I know that would happen in my lifetime.

Ian organised a coach from Catterick to get us to London. On the way down we saw all sorts of vehicles with black and white scarves and pennants fluttering from their windows, all converging on London, like some modern-day pilgrimage.

At motorway service stations, mobile teams of hucksters were selling unofficial, tacky Darlington merchandise, from rosettes at £1 each to flags on flimsy sticks at a fiver apiece.

On arrival at Wembley Way, all you could see were men in Quaker hats or frizzy black and white wigs and little kids with painted faces, waving those yellow foam rubber hands with pointed index fingers that seemed to be popular at that particular time. The moment the team emerged on to the pitch in the blazing sunshine was something I was never going to forget. I'd never seen so many Darlington fans at a game before – there were about 13,000. Not only that, even though we were outnumbered more than two to one by the Plymouth hordes, the 43,431 attendance was a record for a Third Division play-off final at that particular time.

Rather than watching a cup final on television, here I was watching my team, the team I had supported since I was a boy. It was brilliant hearing live, 'Are you watching, Hartlepool!' from the massed ranks of Darlington fans.

As for the game itself, it was a case of missed chances where Darlo were concerned. I can vividly recall, for example, Matty Appleby's shot in the first half going six inches wide of the post. 'If only,' I thought. I did, however, smile at the sight of a male streaker appearing from the Darlington end with a Darlo scarf around his head and hurdling the advertising boards behind the goal before the stewards bundled him away to safety.

But then, in the second half, came the knockout blow when Plymouth's Ronnie Mauge scored with a free header from a corner. And yet, even then, it might not have been all over, when Robbie Painter desperately tried to stretch another six inches to reach a Steve Gaughan cross with the goal at his mercy.

The only blot on that day, apart from the result, was the fact that my good friend John Gray was beaten up outside the stadium by some Plymouth supporters. That was awful, because John is a quiet, inoffensive lad, and has never been a football hooligan in his life.

Although we lost 1-0, I'll never forget the first time I went to Wembley with Darlington.

Even before our Wembley appearance, the team had already started to disintegrate. Appleby had turned down a new contract and was sold to Barnsley for £250,000 in the summer. Gary Bannister retired. Sean Gregan was sold to Preston in February of the following year for £250,000 and Robbie Blake was transferred to Bradford City for £350,000 in March. Once again, it was the same old story of selling the family silver to appease the creditors.

Would the club ever learn?

DARLINGTON V CARDIFF CITY – 1996/97

A new 'saviour' in the shape of Mike Peden took a majority shareholding in the club at the start of the 1996/97 season. His firm, Chaddington Property & Development Co. Ltd, would be responsible for the redevelopment of Feethams.

One of the most memorable matches I attended during that campaign was on 21 October 1996, at home to Cardiff City.

I have to say, though, not because of the football that was on offer that evening. Let me explain.

A new era in the history of the club was inaugurated that night, with the demolition of the old East Stand.

Optimism was rife among the fans that at last the club seemed to be going places.

That evening, the talk in the pub that Ben, the guy who I was with, and I were in was of the demolition and little else.

Once in the ground, we quickly noticed that raffle tickets were selling briskly. The participants could vie for the right to press the red plunger and set off the explosion that would begin the demolition process. I was a bit concerned at the thought of debris falling on the pitch, but it was obvious that any demolition would be largely symbolic, given the fact that Feethams was situated in a residential area. When the moment of the detonation arrived, a compère from the Darlington-based radio station Alpha 103.2 tried to maximise the impact of the event by whipping up the crowd, counting down the seconds like some kind of NASA mission controller.

There was a loud bang, and a row of fireworks along the front of the East Stand spluttered into life, throwing out showers of sparks.

Then the moment we were waiting for finally arrived. A crane hoisted a corrugated-iron panel from the barrel roof and lifted it clear. But that was it. Later, the crane would lower the panel back in position, as if the demolition had been a ghastly mistake! This made the whole event seem positively amateurish in my opinion. Not for the first time in their history, the club had been made to look a complete laughing stock.

The game itself proved to be a similar damp squib and petered out in a dreary 0-0 draw. Perhaps the only noteworthy event was that two Austrians, Mario Dorner and Franz Resch, both signed from Motherwell, made their full debuts for Darlo. Anthony Carss, who had left Darlo for the Bluebirds, played that night and his main contribution was clearing a goalbound shot from Glenn Naylor off the line. This proved to be the only noteworthy action of the whole game.

SOLIHULL BOROUGH V DARLINGTON – FA CUP FIRST-ROUND REPLAY 1996/97

On 26 November 1996 I made the long journey to Hall Green in south Birmingham for this FA Cup first-round replay.

It was a very wet evening when we reached Solihull Borough's Moorlands ground, which they shared with Moor Green FC. To our horror, on entering the stadium, we quickly realised that the away end was uncovered. As a result, I got soaking wet on the terraces, along with the rest of the 500 or so fans in the Darlington contingent.

The game itself turned on the most outrageous refereeing decisions. Uriah Rennie, the official in charge, dished out eight bookings and sent off the Quakers' Lee Turnbull in the 86th minute, for elbowing the Solihull keeper, just after he'd come on as a substitute. Then Mr Rennie remained obstinately deaf to the whistles of the

Darlington fans, even though the 90 minutes were well and truly up.

Despite playing with ten men, we were leading 3-2 with a penalty from Brian Atkinson and goals from former youth team player Paul Robinson and Mario Dorner, yet minute after minute went ticking by with no sign of an end in sight. Solihull eventually got an equaliser 11 minutes into injury time and Mr Rennie played a further minute after that just for good measure.

With the teams level after 30 minutes of extra time, the match then went into a nerve-jangling penalty shoot-out. On this occasion luck was on Darlo's side and they ran out 4-3 victors, with Jason de Vos, our Canadian international defender, scoring the decisive kick. So Ian and I were over the moon that the Quakers were through to the next round. Only just, though.

DARLINGTON V BARNET – 1998/99

The start of the 1998/99 season brought raised expectations for Darlington supporters for the first time in many a year.

Despite the fact that the bookies had made us only 40/1 to win the title, anybody with any sense could see that we would be a force to be reckoned with in the Third Division. Not only did we have an experienced squad of 24 players, but manager David Hodgson, now in his second spell at the club, had also made three very shrewd signings during the close-season: former Middlesbrough central defender Craig Liddle, ex-Sunderland and Derby County striker Marco Gabbiadini and former Manchester City and Sunderland defender Gary Bennett, who assumed the role of player-coach.

At long last, our dilapidated stadium had undergone a much-needed programme of renovation. In the past, this might have entailed no more than the crush barriers receiving a new lick of paint. This time it had been done professionally, a far cry from that farcical episode when the old East Stand was supposedly demolished before the game with Cardiff – its eventual completion the £3m icing on the cake.

To add the finishing touches to our more professional approach, we had acquired a swanky £75,000 coach from Everton to transport the team to away games. Surely, we thought, promotion was just around the corner.

Ben decided to accompany me and Ian to the first game of the season against Barnet and we were able to sample the facilities of the new East Stand for the first time. Incidentally, Ben and I were the first fans to have a pint in the new bar, which was called Strikers. I can remember being very proud about that at the time.

When I started to support Darlo in the early 1970s, Feethams was already beginning to look outmoded and I can testify that it certainly didn't have much space or indeed facilities for disabled fans. With its separate disabled toilet near the main entrance, numerous pitch-level spaces for wheelchair users and good catering facilities, I could certainly have no complaints now on that score. The new East Stand struck me as being one of the best of its kind in the then-named Nationwide League.

As kick-off time approached, the PA announcer said that the start of the game would be delayed by five minutes because of the large crowds waiting to get in. Now that must have been a first for the opening league match of a season.

It seems no one will ever know the true size of the crowd that day. Apparently, the counter on one of the turnstiles ran backwards for a time! The *Northern Echo* said the crowd was 4,200, but in the programme for the next home game the figure was given as 3,450.

From our places in the pitchside disabled area, Ben and I were both intrigued to see former youth team player Carl Pepper warming up with the rest of the squad. When the team was announced over the tannoy, we learned that he was a surprise inclusion at right-back rather than the more experienced Adam Reed, who had just rejoined the club from Premier League side Blackburn Rovers.

When the game did eventually get under way, the two of us witnessed a very good match. Barnet goalkeeper Lee Harrison pulled off a string of tremendous saves to deny Darlo on several occasions and we hit the woodwork as well. Marco Gabbiadini could, and maybe should, have had a hat-trick, but for Harrison's brilliance.

After so much hype and expectation, we were therefore brought back down to earth with a bump by a surprising 2-0 defeat. Nevertheless, despite losing our opening game, Ben, Ian and I were still confident about the season as a whole.

MANSFIELD TOWN V DARLINGTON – 1998/99

Darlington's first game of September 1998 was away to Mansfield Town. I travelled there on the train with a guy called Roger Martin, whom I'm still in contact with to this day.

The two of us changed trains at Sheffield but when we actually arrived the promised assistance to get me off the train wasn't there. The station official apologised and explained that staff at Darlington station hadn't faxed them with the relevant details. Luckily, a young woman with a pushchair helped Roger to lift my wheelchair off the train, which was very kind of her.

We then continued on our journey to Worksop and finally arrived in Mansfield, where we had planned to meet fellow Darlo fan Karl Alexander, who comes from Colchester. Digressing slightly, an amusing story about Karl springs to mind.

Let me explain. Rumour has it that he once saw Colchester United, his hometown club, get beat by Darlo so he decided that because the Quakers were the better team on the day, he'd follow them instead and he has done so ever since. As with Roger, I'm still in contact with Karl to this day.

Anyway, back to my story, and eventually Karl turned up at a pub near the ground called the Early Doors, along with Brian Elsey and Trevor Rutter from Sheffield. As we relaxed over our drinks, we got chatting to some Mansfield fans about their chairman and discussed the case of Steve Whitehall, their centre-forward, who had been sold to Oldham Athletic because he wasn't being paid by his club. In fact, it emerged during our conversation that the PFA had been paying the Mansfield players' wages for quite a while.

Upon entering the ground, Roger and I discovered that both ends behind the goals had been cordoned off for safety reasons – hence no fans were allowed in those areas. This robbed the match of much of its atmosphere to say the least.

During the early part of the game, referee Tony Leake sustained a knee injury and was replaced in the 16th minute by his assistant, Neil Hancox. Fortunately, he proved to be an able deputy.

The match was settled when Marco Gabbiadini, who earlier had a goal disallowed for offside, sent a low shot past goalkeeper Ian Bowling in the 33rd minute. 'No trouble at Mill as Darlington march on' wrote the *Northern Echo* reporter in his match report the following Monday. The win left Darlington's promotion train firmly on track.

After the game, Roger, Karl and I went for a drink in the supporters' club bar. Again we chatted to some

Mansfield fans who, to a man, admitted that Darlo were the better team on the day and looked like genuine promotion contenders. These remarks were certainly pleasing to hear, especially as they came from opposition supporters. From there we had a few more pints in a pub near the station and caught the train home, arriving back in Darlington at around ten o'clock.

One final comment: this was the first time I'd gone to a match with Roger, and I can honestly say that I really enjoyed my day out with him.

DARLINGTON V BURNLEY – FA CUP FIRST ROUND 1998/99

The first round of the FA Cup provided some distraction from our league campaign. The draw had given the Quakers a home tie against Second Division Burnley. However, the Feethams pitch was totally unplayable, so our neighbours Middlesbrough stepped forward and kindly offered use of the Riverside Stadium to host the tie – a generous gesture by their chairman Steve Gibson. The game took place on Tuesday, 17 November. I made the short journey to Teesside with Ian in his car.

A crowd of 5,059 were at the Riverside and they saw Darlo make a strong start, forcing four corners in the first quarter of an hour with Glenn Naylor going closest to a goal with a header from one of them that went just wide. Burnley seemed quite happy to soak up the pressure and rely on counter-attacks and it nearly paid off in the 16th minute when their most dangerous player, Glen Little, beat two men with a strong run but his enticing cross was cut out by Mark Barnard, who conceded a corner. Two minutes later Marco Gabbiadini went close with a shot from the edge of the box which visiting keeper Frank-Petter Kval did well to save and then a minute later he made an even better save from a Gabbiadini header. Burnley hit back and Steve Morgan clipped the bar with a header from a Little corner.

At the end of the half it was Darlington who threatened when Darren Roberts forced his way into the box but had his shot blocked by Kval. However, the deadlock was broken in the 37th minute when the visitors grabbed the lead. Quakers centre-half Steve Tutill lost the ball on the halfway line and it fell to Burnley full-back Phil Eastwood, who played it forward for former Middlesbrough striker Andy Payton to advance and easily beat David Preece.

Darlington began the second half in determined fashion. Brian Atkinson had a shot deflected wide and then Gabbiadini fired high over when in a good position. Burnley thought they'd increased their lead in the 53rd minute when Payton netted again but this time it was ruled out for offside.

The striker was booked for disputing the decision. They did, however, double their lead two minutes later with a controversial penalty when Payton went down under a challenge from Craig Liddle just inside the box.

The referee saw nothing wrong and waved play on, but his assistant flagged and a penalty was awarded. Payton smashed home the resulting spot kick.

The Quakers kept pressing forward. Striker Mario Dorner replaced defender Gary Bennett and very nearly scored with his first touch, a right-footed shot that just cleared the bar. Atkinson then hit a powerful shot which was blocked and Naylor followed up but Kval somehow scrambled his effort around the post. The game changed in the 73rd minute. Liddle played a back pass to Preece and as he cleared the ball Payton went in late on the keeper and earned his second booking. Although two goals to the good, Burnley had to play the last 17 minutes with ten men.

Darlington got back into the game in the 80th minute. Naylor was pushed in the back by Brian Reid as they contested a cross from Michael Oliver and Brian Atkinson coolly converted the resulting penalty. The Quakers were completely on top now and Burnley were hanging on for their lives. Dorner's chip went just over the bar, then Gabbiadini blazed another shot too high, but in the 86th minute they got a deserved equaliser. A cross from the right by Gabbiadini was headed into the box by Oliver, touched back by Naylor and smashed into the net by Dorner from 12 yards out. Adam Reed had a header cleared off the line and then as the game entered stoppage time, Darlington grabbed a dramatic winner. Oliver won a tackle 30 yards out and the ball ran to Dorner just outside the penalty area. He squared it to the corner of the box where the onrushing Mark Barnard hit a first-time shot across the keeper just inside the far post. From two down with ten minutes left, Darlo had fought back to secure a famous victory.

Ian and I couldn't believe what we had just witnessed as we made our way back home and were pleased that we were present to see an absolutely fantastic performance from our team.

CAMBRIDGE UNITED V DARLINGTON – 1998/99

In November 1998, Darlo were away at Cambridge United. Ian couldn't go, so I decided to go on my own (I arranged for Stephen to meet me on the train when it stopped at Ely) having booked assistance in advance from GNER. Since this was the first time that I'd travelled unaccompanied on a journey that involved changing trains, it goes without saying that I was a bit wary.

I caught the half past eight train and a railway official met me on the platform at Peterborough on my arrival with a ramp. As I had a good half-hour wait before catching my connection, I decided to go for a coffee in the snack bar to kill time; rather surprisingly there weren't any more Darlo fans around, which I thought was unusual.

When my connecting train arrived, the same station official put me on board to complete my journey to Cambridge. During the trip, I bought two cans of lager which I drank in order to whet my appetite for the day ahead.

On arrival at Ely, Stephen got on board as arranged and we both continued our journey on to Cambridge.

We arrived at our destination about 11.30am where we then met up with John Wilson and Mark Trenholme, both Darlo fans living in the south of England. We had a few pints in pubs in the high street, including the Green Man, the Haymakers, the Dog & Pheasant and the Five Bells. While on our pub trek, we bumped into John Gray and Richard Jones. John said that I could have gone on the train with them, rather than me travelling on my own. It was nice of him to offer, but I told him that I needed to find out for myself whether I could manage such a journey unaccompanied). Richard regaled us with the fact that Cambridge's heaviest defeat and indeed heaviest win were against Darlo – both 6-0 scorelines. 'Even Nick Hornby saw Darlo play and lose 4-0 against Cambridge in his book *Fever Pitch*,' I retorted. Richard seemed genuinely surprised by this fact.

For a change, we arrived well before the start of the match; a rare event for John, since nine times out of ten he manages to miss the kick-off at away games, despite more often than not arriving in the town concerned at around opening time. But that is John for you. He won't change now, that's for sure.

After buying some programmes, we all took our places in the away end.

Interestingly, for all those 'anoraks' reading this, this was the first time that the new fluorescent yellow balls were used in the Football League.

At half-time, with Darlo leading 1-0 through a peach of a goal from Glenn Naylor, Stephen kindly decided to treat me to a burger, but after biting into it I soon wished that he hadn't bothered. It was one of those horrid tinned specimens, which had been boiled rather than fried or grilled. After just the one bite, I quickly disposed of it by dropping it on the end of Stephen's boot! Fortunately, the remains of it ended up far enough from me meaning that I didn't have to suffer the stench during the second half.

During the interval, defender Steve Tutill, who had been bleeding profusely after a clash of heads, had six stitches inserted in a head wound.

As the teams re-emerged I expected to see a further battle if we were to come away with a result. Even when John Taylor levelled in the 57th minute, the game looked to be heading for a draw until Adam Reed headed past his own keeper in the 79th minute, making the final score 2-1 to Cambridge.

After the game, Stephen and I said our goodbyes to the lads and then set off on a pub crawl around Cambridge, once again visiting the Green Man and the Haymakers. At around seven we left Cambridge by train and headed for Ely, where we decided to stay in a pub called the Prince Albert in the middle of the city centre, and we talked at length about the game – and about striker Glenn Naylor in particular. We both agreed that he was an underrated player who would always reach double figures during a season. He joined Darlo in 1995 from York, and since then had been a fairly regular goalscorer. While chatting and reminiscing, we downed several pints.

On leaving the Prince Albert, we decided to get a taxi to Coventry where Stephen lived. Unfortunately, with us both being rather the worse for wear, I slipped while being put into the car and banged the side of my head on the taxi door. In next to no time there was blood everywhere and my shirt resembled Steve Tutill's. It turned out that my ear had been nicked and that accounted for the amount of blood. To compound matters, due to the shock of the fall, this triggered off a spasm attack, which involved me shaking from head to foot. Stephen immediately panicked and tried to insist on taking me to a hospital, but I refused point-blank. Once we arrived at Stephen's house, he cleaned up my ear and eventually my spasms ceased.

The following day, Stephen insisted on coming with me on the train as far as Peterborough to make sure that I was all right. It was good of him, but luckily I was back to normal and had an uneventful journey back to Darlington.

DARLINGTON V CHESTER CITY – 1998/99

By February 1999 fans' suspicions regarding Mike Peden were aroused by means of an article written by him in the matchday programme against Mansfield Town.

The article was a strenuous rebuttal concerning accusations of financial irregularities, made by Chris Hardy, the editor of the fanzine *Darlo: It's Just Like Watching Brazil*.

In his article, Mr Peden vigorously denied any wrongdoing. However, I had long been concerned about the club's finances, ever since the sale of star defender Jason de Vos to Dundee United earlier in the season.

April brought further rumours that Peden was on the verge of resigning and was to be replaced by millionaire businessman George Reynolds, and also that the players hadn't received their wages, not for the first time.

By this time the club was heavily in debt and everyone knew that something would have to give sooner or later. The new stand (so we heard) had been mortgaged to the hilt and now Darlo were struggling to keep up with the repayments.

Our first match of May was at home to Chester City. On entering the ground, supporters were saying that Mike Peden had left and that George Reynolds was about to take over.

Outside the bar, Ben and I saw Reynolds's Rolls-Royce with its personalised number plate which rather gave the game away as to his intentions.

Before the kick-off, everyone inside the bar was buzzing about the imminent takeover. Rumour had it that this would happen within the next week or so.

During the match the Darlo fans started singing 'There's only one Georgie Reynolds' as he took his seat in the directors' box. Interestingly, Peden was conspicuous by his absence.

Unfortunately, Darlo's display didn't match the mood of the crowd and they produced by far their worst performance of the season, eventually losing 2-1 to what can only be described as a poor Chester side with Glenn Naylor scoring the hosts' only goal.

DARLINGTON V EXETER CITY – 1998/99

Because of the rumours circulating that an important announcement was going to be made regarding the ownership of the club, Ian, Ben and I made our way straight to the ground to witness this match, rather than go to the pub first.

When Mr Reynolds strode on to the pitch, accompanied by his wife Susan, they were both holding Darlington scarves aloft, much to the delight of the Tin Shed faithful.

Using a microphone, he stated that he would pay off the club's debts of almost £4m. He added that his takeover would be sealed by midday the following Wednesday. 'The deal is on,' he said. He vowed to pay monies owed to backroom staff and players totalling

£90,000 and also promised to invest in new players and build a new stadium with a 25,000 capacity. 'I know there will be some Doubting Thomases, but I promise you I will deliver the goods for Darlington,' were his final words.

The Quakers actually played really well that night, especially in the second half, but to my amazement, no one was watching the game – as they were all looking towards the directors' box. It was something I had never personally witnessed in all the years I had been watching football, and I have never seen such a thing again to this day.

Darlington won at a canter 4-0 with goals from Gary Bennett and a hat-trick from Marco Gabbiadini, who became the first player to score three goals in a league match at Feethams in ten years.

Mr Reynolds had now seen two sides of Darlington in just three days – the worst performance and the best.

In the bar afterwards, everyone was talking about gaining promotion the following season. I decided to wait and see. After all, I'd seen plenty of chairmen come and go in the time I'd supported Darlington.

I later read in the *Northern Echo* that Mike Peden had severed all his links with the club. In fact, he wasn't even involved in the negotiations with George Reynolds, since executive director Bernard Lowery had conducted them on his behalf. This represented an ignominious end for the Midlands-based entrepreneur who had vowed to lead the club to bigger and better things when he took over in 1997.

The building of the new East Stand was supposed to have been a symbol of Darlo's bright new future. However, instead, it had become a financial millstone around the club's neck, eventually leading to financial ruin and near extinction.

ROCHDALE V DARLINGTON – 1999/2000

Since George Reynolds had assumed control of the club, I witnessed further activity in the transfer market during the close-season which saw manager David Hodgson bring in players of real quality for the level they were playing at. They included veteran Neil Aspin (formerly of Leeds United and Port Vale), midfielder Martin Gray (ex-Sunderland and Oxford United), Welsh international forward Lee Nogan (Grimsby Town) and pacy winger Neil Heaney (Manchester City). Not surprisingly, the bookies had made us 5-1 to win the title.

Darlo started off the season like a steam train, winning their first three games. With optimism being really high, George Reynolds decided to call a supporters' club forum at Feethams. Ben and I decided to attend. When George entered the room, he spotted me immediately and said, 'Hello, Flipper,' referencing my nickname with the Darlington fans.

He then regaled us with his visit to Halifax for the first match of the season. At the gate was a jobsworth official.

'Can I get a drink somewhere?' asked George, lowering the electric window of his chauffeur-driven Rolls-Royce. 'No,' said the official. 'There's no kettle.' 'Can I have some food then?' said George. 'No,' said the official. 'Where do I park?' asked George. 'Don't know,' said the man. All the while George mimicked his broad Yorkshire accent. As George stepped from his vehicle and strode towards the nearest door the man interjected once more, 'You can't go in there pal, this lounge is for the directors' wives.' As a parting shot the man said, 'Tha's come 'ere to get beat.' 'We'll see,' replied George, confidently.

After the game, which we won 1-0, George asked, 'Can I go over to the fans?' 'No,' said the same official. 'In that case, if you don't let me go over to them the fans'll come over to me.' 'OK,' said the official.

Then George talked about another one of our recent opponents, Bolton Wanderers. Their manager, Colin Todd, had swaggered into the ground and boasted, 'We're a former Premiership club. Our players cost millions of pounds.' When they arrived at the club they marched in with an air of supreme confidence and superiority. They entered almost disdainfully. George imitated their haughty bearing.

When the game was over their heads were downcast as they clambered on board their coach. So much for their misplaced confidence.

George was wound up by now, relishing his role of comedian and impromptu entertainer. You could tell that he was a born showman, the sort to grace a circus or fairground.

Like a kid with a new toy, he unveiled his plans for the new stadium. He took the rolled-up drawings from a cardboard tube and then held them aloft and walked among the fans.

Then he rounded on the protestors, who were opposed to the project; though he did stress that everything had been done to minimise the adverse effect of the scheme on the local residents.

At this point I interjected and said that I wanted to be able to buy a season ticket if I so wished in the East Stand, not the Tin Shed. I didn't want to be considered a charity case. This received a round of applause from the fans in attendance. However, my idea was never acted upon, so I decided to sponsor a player instead.

George then let the fans in on his master plan, which involved pinching supporters from Middlesbrough, Sunderland and Newcastle to fill the new stadium. His aim was to attract 5,000 from each club. He also went on to say that it would cost £10 for a seat, and only a fiver behind either one of the goals, as he wanted to bring football back into the price range of the average working family. As a result, he said that the cost of a ticket would be pegged.

To illustrate his point, he told us about his chipboard business when he had undercut his competitors. That was what he wanted to do with football. By bringing the prices down, he hoped that this would encourage more people to go to the games.

George explained that he wanted Feethams to be used by local youngsters for sporting events. It would be his gift to the community.

Local journalist Ray Simpson was at the forum that evening and Ben later spoke to him in the toilets. Ray frankly admitted that he couldn't use a lot of the material heard that night because it was just too controversial.

George ended the proceedings with an amusing comment about our former goalkeeper, David Preece. Having been sold to Aberdeen for £200,000 a few weeks prior, Preece had just let in six goals against Celtic. According to George, it was a good job we had received the money for him already otherwise we might have got him back with a note attached saying 'return to sender!'

The two of us left the forum in optimistic mood after this tour de force one-man show from our charismatic new owner.

Anyway, back to matters on the pitch. In September 1999, I went to Rochdale with Ian and Ben in Ian's car.

Outside the stadium, Ian had an argument with a club official as to where he should park his car. 'Is he all there?' I asked rather too loudly, annoyed by the man's condescending attitude. Both Ian and Ben told me to be quiet. After a few choice words, and showing him my wheelchair which was still in the boot, he eventually allowed us to park in a disabled bay. Before I had the chance to get out of the car, a woman appeared and then got rather stroppy with us, saying that we couldn't park there. Ben didn't think she was really convinced that I was disabled, despite the fact that the official had already seen my wheelchair. We didn't have an orange badge to display in the windscreen because I'd left it at home. Ian was annoyed by now and asked, 'Do you want to see the wheelchair as well?'

After wasting so much valuable drinking time arguing the toss with the two 'Little Hitlers', we headed straight to the Church pub near the ground and sat outside in the beer garden overlooking a bowling green.

Interestingly, the barman remembered me from the previous season – he even brought me a bottle of Budweiser without me having to queue for it. A very nice gesture, I thought. Once inside the ground, Ben took me to the disabled area, where fellow disabled Darlo fan Terry Soley sat next to me. However, Ben was prevented by a steward from standing beside me so he took a seat in the front row of the Main Stand.

The first half was largely uneventful until the dismissal of Rochdale defender Keith Hill for a second bookable offence, a foul on Marco Gabbiadini.

Despite the fact that Dale had been reduced to ten men, it was actually Darlo who were under the cosh for much of the second period. An old couple sitting behind me, supporting Darlo, whinged constantly about the team, the referee, in fact just about everything.

Nevertheless, after we managed to secure a 0-0 draw, I just shook my head in disbelief at their constant moaning. We were third in the league for God's sake. Maybe they should have cast their minds back to the 1970s when the club was always struggling to avoid re-election. They would have had something to moan about then.

GILLINGHAM V DARLINGTON – FA CUP SECOND ROUND 1999/2000

For this match I travelled on my own by train and was met at King's Cross by Brian Elsey, who then accompanied me for the second leg of my journey. On arrival at Gillingham, we were met by John Wilson and Mark Trenholme. The four of us made our way to The Will Adams for a quick drink (we didn't have as much time as we normally did, as the game kicked off at 1pm) before heading for the ground.

When we arrived at the main entrance, despite the fact that I'd rung the club the day before, we were told that there wasn't any room for wheelchairs. Brian demanded to see the head steward. There were three people, including me, in wheelchairs waiting to gain admittance to the ground. All of us had booked our spaces in advance. By now it was quarter past one and we were still waiting for the head steward to make an appearance. When he did arrive he said that some seats had been taken out of the front of the stand and that we could get into the game. He asked us for £10 each, which he promptly put into his pocket. To be honest, I was disgusted by the whole episode. Brian told him exactly what he thought of him in no uncertain terms, and we eventually got into the ground at 25 past one.

Darlo were awful and were 2-0 down at half-time. We were missing the suspended Marco Gabbiadini. One of Darlo's other main forwards, Jesper Hjorth, was only on the bench.

Gillingham added a third just after the break, with the dangerous Bob Taylor getting his second goal of the day. We managed a consolation goal through Peter Duffield. After the disappointing Lee Nogan was brought off and replaced by Hjorth midway through the second half, things livened up and we created some chances. However, 3-1 was the final score and we were out of the FA Cup.

ASTON VILLA V DARLINGTON – FA CUP THIRD ROUND 1999/2000

After Darlo were beaten at Gillingham, I thought our cup adventure was over for another season. How wrong I was.

After Manchester United had decided to withdraw from the competition in order to take part in the Club World Championship, the Football Association, in its ultimate wisdom, came up with the novel idea of including the names of all the teams who had been knocked out in the second round. From these clubs a so-called 'lucky loser' would be drawn in order to fill the vacant space in round three.

Since George Reynolds had often claimed to have a personal hotline to God, was it any wonder that Darlo were pulled out of the hat? Not only that, but we were also handed a plum money-spinning draw away trip to Aston Villa, a game that I attended with Ben.

The two of us caught a train at about eight o'clock in the morning, arriving in Birmingham New Street station at about 11.30am following an uneventful journey.

Since you had to go up an escalator to exit the station, we had no other choice but to ask an official to take us under the platform – it was very wet down there, with pools of dirty, standing water, like some underground cavern. Then we went up in a service lift which took us to the exit.

After having a few drinks in a pub near the station, The Shakespeare, we headed back to New Street only to find out that our train was about to leave. So the pair of us went through the barrier and made our way to the platform, only to be confronted by a steep flight of steps.

Fortunately, a policeman happened to be in the vicinity and he gave Ben a hand in carrying the wheelchair up the steps. This wasn't the end of our problems since we now realised that because the waiting train had very old carriages with narrow doors, these were not wide enough to get a wheelchair through them. If we were going to get on board, I would have to travel in the guard's van.

Luckily, the policeman was a gentleman and helped us by radioing for assistance. The guard, who turned up very quickly, soon had the doors open for us and I was safely stowed inside.

It was very hot inside there but Ben was at least able to rest and sit down on a seat. In any event, it was only two stops along the line – the train's first stop was Aston then Witton. But our trials and tribulations were far from over.

The pair of us were horrified to find that Witton station was in the process of modernisation. Although this was a good thing in itself, and there would eventually be a new wheelchair-friendly ramp leading down to street level, the only problem was that the work wasn't finished, so we had to get some assistance from the station officials to manhandle me and my wheelchair down two flights of temporary steps.

By then it had also started to rain quite heavily, so the metal steps were slippery underfoot, and I was nearly tipped out of my chair on more than one occasion. Fortunately, we made it to the bottom in one piece.

We reached the ground only to come up against yet more trouble. We were led inside only to be taken back from where we had come and into another entrance to the disabled area.

Although Ben had paid for a seat in the away end he had to accompany me and sit near the corner flag where he could hardly see the game. He was annoyed by this and moved further along to the ordinary seats where he could get a better view.

During the game, a Brummie policeman on duty behind me moaned constantly about the standard of football on offer – mind you, he was a Birmingham City fan.

There were also some Cardiff City fans in front of Ben cheering for Villa. As their game against Bolton Wanderers had been called off, it seemed as if they had come simply to cause trouble by winding up the Darlo fans.

Darlington lost a thrilling game 2-1, Paul Heckingbottom scoring our only goal by slotting in the rebound after England international goalkeeper David James had saved Peter Duffield's penalty.

After the game, the two of us went to the Yew Tree pub where we had a couple of pints before ordering a cab to New Street, not wishing to repeat our experiences at Witton.

HARTLEPOOL UNITED V DARLINGTON – PLAY-OFF SEMI-FINAL FIRST LEG 1999/2000

During April and May of 2000, Darlington's form slumped, culminating in finishing in a final league position of fourth and therefore missing out on automatic promotion. This meant the club had to once again endure the drama of the play-offs.

We were paired against our fiercest rivals Hartlepool United, who had finished seventh, and the first leg would be at Victoria Park. The two remaining teams were Peterborough United and Barnet who would contest the other semi-final.

Ben and I travelled up to Hartlepool on the 11 o'clock train, changing at Thornaby. Having bought a copy of the *Northern Echo* from the newsagents at the station, one article in particular caught our eye. According to the report, George Reynolds had recently been mugged and his Rolex watch stolen while visiting London. Given his reputation as a hardman, we thought the thieves must have been either high on drugs or very, very stupid.

By the time we had finished the paper, the train was pulling into Hartlepool station. As we had plenty of time to kill we decided to keep a low profile in one of the town-centre pubs before making our way to the ground.

The game was not without its moments of controversy. One of the first talking points was in the fifth minute when Craig Liddle brought down former Darlo trainee James Coppinger as he was heading towards goal. Luckily, the referee, Barry Knight, only showed our centre-half a yellow card. In the 35th minute we were again grateful to Mr Knight as Liddle settled our nerves by blasting home the ball from close range with a right-footed shot.

The game ebbed and flowed until the 76th minute when we were awarded a controversial penalty after Glenn

Naylor theatrically threw himself to the ground after the most innocuous contact with United's keeper Martin Hollund, who was red-carded for the offence. Once again, we were thankful for Mr Knight's interpretation of the events. The first task that substitute goalkeeper Andy Dibble had to do was to pick the ball out of the net after Marco Gabbiadini converted the penalty. So, given what had happened to George Reynolds in London you could say that we also mugged Hartlepool that particular day.

After the second goal was scored, the home supporters spat at and pelted David Hodgson with coins, one of which, a 50p piece, struck him on the back of the head. I was disgusted to see football fans behaving like that and felt that he should have had more protection from the stewards than he received.

After the final whistle sounded, we heard later that, as the players were leaving the pitch, Gabbiadini was punched by an irate Hartlepool fan as he made his way towards the tunnel.

Once again, there appeared to be no protection from the Hartlepool stewards, something that I personally just couldn't comprehend. The two of us had left the ground by then in order to avoid any trouble that may occur outside and Ben pushed me in the direction of the railway station by a circuitous route.

We then went into a pub near the station as there were police vans in the area. It would have been madness to catch the early train, so we decided to bide our time and have a couple of pints.

Suddenly, the pub filled up and all around us were Hartlepool fans. It goes without saying that they didn't know we supported Darlo because my replica shirt was carefully hidden inside my tightly zipped-up jacket. We both sniggered to ourselves as we watched a police dog van pull up outside.

From the safety of the pub, we witnessed several charges like those of the Light Brigade as some Darlo fans tried to get at the home supporters. The two Alsatians caged in the back of the police van appeared eager to see action. In the end the police grew tired of the skirmishing and let the dogs out – this had the desired effect.

While all hell was breaking out in the street, a Hartlepool fan in the pub, who was tattooed with HUFC on the back of his neck, commented, 'I wish there were some f***ing Darlo fans in here,' to which Ben and I just sat there smirking between ourselves.

Once the fun and games had subsided, and the police dogs had been exercised on their leashes, things calmed down when the bulk of the Darlo supporters left on the first available train.

We still remained behind in the pub with our new-found 'friends' and when the coast was clear, Ben pushed me over the road to the station where we caught the next train to Thornaby and, shortly after, another to Darlington.

DARLINGTON V HARTLEPOOL UNITED – PLAY-OFF SEMI-FINAL SECOND LEG 1999/2000

For the return leg, I met Ben in the Dalesman, a pub near the ground, having gone there straight from work. Despite the fact that it was only around half past five, we were both surprised to discover that the main doors had been locked and we had to knock on the side door to gain entry.

The pair of us were shocked to see that the pub was full of Darlo fans, despite the fact it was still early. Since we had come straight from work we both opted to have a meal.

While we were waiting for the food to arrive, we chatted about the forthcoming match. We were both confident that we would win the tie overall, since no side had scored more than two goals at Feethams all that season. The omens were therefore good. However, Ben pointed out that there was always a first time for everything.

From there we went to Strikers where we had arranged to meet Ian. The bar was really full and by the time Ian queued to get some drinks it was almost time to leave. Ben therefore pushed me into the disabled area, with me only having drank half of my pint, not that it mattered in the scheme of things.

Darlo scored early through a Gary Strodder own goal in the ninth minute, virtually killing the tie off as a contest. The rest of the match was really just a stroll in the park as Hartlepool didn't really look like scoring.

At the final whistle, to add to the air of celebration the tannoy played 'Que Sera Sera' and 'Perfect Day' by Lou Reed. Darlo were on their way to Wembley again for the second time in four years.

DARLINGTON V PETERBOROUGH UNITED – PLAY-OFF FINAL AT WEMBLEY 1999/2000

Ben and I travelled to London for the final against Peterborough United by train on the Friday morning as the match had been rescheduled for that night due to the fact that England were playing a friendly against Brazil the following day. This was not ideal for either team and would mean a slightly lower crowd than would have normally been expected.

Nevertheless, we decided to travel early and had already arranged to stay overnight in accommodation that Ben had booked near the stadium, returning on the Saturday afternoon.

On arrival, in London, we caught a black cab off the rank outside King's Cross station to our bed and breakfast on Forty Lane near Wembley Stadium. Because of the heavy lunchtime traffic it took an eternity for us to arrive at our destination and the fare was an obscene £46! I still think to this day that the driver took us that particular route in order to be able to charge as much as he could.

When the cab arrived outside the B&B, the pair of us had to ransack our pockets in order to raise sufficient cash to pay the fare.

Our state of annoyance was compounded when Ben had great difficulty in getting my wheelchair through the door to our room. We both found this rather surprising considering the fact that the accommodation was supposed to be disabled-friendly.

Once inside, we also discovered that there was a high step up into the toilet and shower room. It would have been impossible for Ben to get me in there so I ended up having to use the toilet and bathroom near the B&B's entrance along the corridor. I found this particularly frustrating, as the owner had assured Ben when he had booked it that the room was 'perfectly accessible'. However, I decided against complaining as we were only going to be staying one night and it wouldn't have been worth the hassle.

After we had dropped off our belongings and got our key, we went for a wander in the rain along Forty Lane towards the local supermarket. As a matter of priority we had to use the cashpoint to withdraw some more money, as we had already overspent due to the taxi debacle. We then had a coffee and a snack in the restaurant.

Since it was still raining heavily we decided to catch a taxi to a pub called JJ Moons in Kingsbury near the tube station, where we had arranged to meet some of the Darlo fans who lived in the London area. This time, though, the fare was only a fiver.

Just as we finished our first pint, Stephen arrived, closely followed by other southern-based Darlo fans John and Beverley Wilson.

After leaving the pub, Ben pushed me along a very rain-swept Wembley Way, along with the rest of our group. The rain was incessant and didn't relent all evening.

On entering the stadium, our friends left us to get to their seats and at the same time a steward issued us both with a plastic cape, which certainly came in handy and kept us dry.

It was ironic that we ended up having to play this important fixture on a water-sodden surface that resembled the Feethams pitch at its worst. Ben and I both felt that the game should really have been called off in the circumstances.

As the players entered the arena, a firework display exploded into life as the PA blasted out 'We Will Rock You' by Queen and 'Roll With It' by Oasis.

The rain seemed to dampen the whole occasion. Also, I was both disappointed and surprised to see that the team had been tinkered with and Phil Brumwell, who put in two excellent performances against Hartlepool United in the semi-finals, had been dropped to the bench and replaced by Neil Aspin in a reshaped Darlington defence.

After the national anthem was played, the fans behind me broke into a spontaneous chorus of, 'We love you Darlo, we do … Oh Darlo we love you'. Darlington's

10,000 fans certainly made plenty of noise but were outsung by the 20,000 Peterborough contingent. The reason for the overwhelming odds as far as the number of supporters representing each team was concerned was that Peterborough is only one stop away from King's Cross by train and supporters could attend the game straight from work, whereas the Darlo fans would have had to take at least an afternoon off. Had it been a Saturday match, I felt that the numbers would have been much more even.

My own feeling was that we could win due to the fact that we had beaten Peterborough 2-0 at Feethams only a few weeks previously and in Marco Gabbiadini we had a forward who inspired fear in the opposition and could win any game through his own individual brilliance.

The two of us witnessed a spirited performance by Darlo in the first half. In the first minute the Quakers almost took the lead after Michael Oliver crossed into the box for Gabbiadini to head just wide from the penalty spot. Gabbiadini had another chance in the tenth minute when he sent a Peter Duffield cross just wide from ten yards out. Three minutes later he had yet another opportunity but the ball was deflected by a Peterborough defender for a corner. 'Are you watching, Hartlepool?' sang the fans as we turned the screw on our opponents. By this time, Ben and I had a gut feeling that it wasn't going to be our night. This was further compounded when Duffield hit the post in the 26th minute.

Following the half-time interval, Darlo yet again could and maybe should have scored when Neil Heaney had a dangerous shot blocked by a Peterborough defender. In the 64th minute Darlington had to reshuffle their defence after left-back Paul Heckingbottom went off injured to be replaced by forward Glenn Naylor, with Oliver slotting into Heckingbottom's position. Although Oliver was a left-sided midfielder he wasn't a genuine left-back.

Our fears became a reality when in the 70th minute Steve Castle headed the ball into the Darlo box for former Wimbledon star Andy Clarke to have a shot blocked by Andy Collett. However, Clarke pounced on the rebound to volley home which led to Peterborough manager Barry Fry sprinting down the touchline in celebration. My reaction was to put my head in my hands as at that moment I realised that Darlo would not be going up and all David Hodgson's hard work had counted for nothing. After the goal, both teams missed several good chances as we pushed forward looking for the equaliser which never came.

Darlo had been unlucky as they had missed numerous chances, not for the first time that season, which had ultimately cost them the match.

One event that made us think that Gabbiadini might be leaving the club was when he took off his shirt at the end and threw it towards one of the Darlo fans. This struck us as a gesture of farewell.

After the game we went to a pub called The Crock of Gold where we had to endure the highlights of the game on the television in the midst of jubilant Peterborough fans. We saw the post-match interviews with managers Hodgson and Fry. The former was drained but gracious in defeat, the latter his usual ebullient self.

The following day during our train journey home, Ben and I started to chat as the reality of what had happened the night before began to sink in. We wondered what the consequences of not achieving promotion would be. The two of us hoped that the nucleus of the team would be kept together and a few new faces would be added to the squad. I personally thought that if this were to be the case then the club would easily achieve promotion the following season.

On the plus side, we both agreed that Darlo had a good goalkeeper in Andy Collett but needed to sign a better backup than Mark Samways or Chris Porter. We also had a solid defence but, unfortunately, Martin Gray apart, the central midfield players were weak and needed replacing.

We had flair in abundance on the left flank, through Neil Heaney, and with Neil Wainwright returning to Sunderland we were reliant on centre-forward Jesper Hjorth filling his boots. Again, this needed to be remedied if we wanted to go up.

Finally, up front we were too reliant upon the individual skills of Gabbiadini and needed to find the correct partner for our top scorer, who had been named the Third Division Player of the Year. Duffield was the best foil for Gabbiadini, out of a pretty inconsistent bunch.

We therefore concluded that we needed a backup goalkeeper, two central midfield players, a right-winger and a forward, or two if Gabbiadini left. This could have been achieved by releasing players who we felt were not up to the job, freeing up wages to bring in better replacements.

On arrival in Darlington, we left the train wondering what the summer would bring for our club.

We didn't have to wait long to find out.

4

The 2000s

DARLINGTON V NOTTINGHAM FOREST – LEAGUE CUP FIRST ROUND FIRST LEG 2000/01

The 2000/01 season kicked off with Gary Bennett at the helm after another summer of turmoil at Darlington Football Club. After that play-off defeat at Wembley by Peterborough, the summer of 2000 saw the break-up of the team that had so nearly clinched promotion. A reduced wage bill saw the departure of regular first-teamers Marco Gabbiadini, Neil Heaney, Peter Duffield, Michael Oliver and Steve Tutill.

Then, just ten days before the start of the new season, manager David Hodgson walked away following yet another clash with George Reynolds, this time after the chairman made public all the players' wages and bonus payments. Reserve team manager Bennett was immediately installed as the new boss.

The season began with two 1-1 draws, against Rochdale and Exeter City, and then attention switched to the League Cup. Darlington had been paired with Nottingham Forest in the first round. Forest had been relegated from the Premier League in 1998/99 and were rebuilding their team under player-manager David Platt. They still had several players from their Premier League days and so would provide a stiff test for Bennett's team.

I watched this match with Ian from my regular spot in the East Stand. The home side were forced into changes as they'd started the season with Lee Nogan and new Dutch signing Tom Kaak in partnership up front, but they were both carrying knocks and missed the Forest game. Their places were taken by Jesper Hjorth and local youngster Gary Williamson, who made his first start for the club after coming through the youth team. Brian Atkinson missed the game due to tendonitis on his knee and Bennett also chose to rest goalkeeper Andy Collett, to give a debut to another Dutch capture, Frank van der Geest.

A crowd of 4,724 turned out at Feethams on 22 August to see Darlo make a promising start to the first leg. Williamson turned and fired straight at visiting goalkeeper Dave Beasant and in their next attack Craig Liddle glanced a header across the face of goal and just wide. Darlington took the lead in the 15th minute. Chris Bart-Williams had an attempted back pass into his own box intercepted by the alert Williamson who was upended by Tony Vaughan. With regular penalty taker Atkinson missing from the side, Stuart Elliott took on the responsibility and easily beat Beasant.

The lead only lasted for five minutes, however, when Gary Himsworth tripped Vaughan in the box and Bart-Williams stepped forward to confidently convert the penalty for the Forest equaliser. Two minutes later the visitors almost took the lead when Stern John cleverly worked his way into the box but fired straight at Van der Geest. In an entertaining game, Darlo continued to create opportunities and Elliott nearly claimed his second with a 30-yarder that flew just past the post, then Martin Gray hit a powerful drive that Beasant just managed to hold on to, diving to his right. Forest always looked dangerous and went close to a second just before half-time when Van der Geest saved with his foot from a close-range Marlon Harewood effort, with Liddle doing well to block the follow-up from Gary Jones.

Darlington started the second period brightly and went close in the 49th minute. A Gray cross from the left was only inches away from the unmarked Williamson at the far post, and a minute later it was Williamson again who was denied his first senior goal by a good save from Beasant, diving at the foot of his post. Hjorth was substituted after 58 minutes and replaced by Mark Angel, who lined up on the wing, allowing Glenn Naylor to move up front into Hjorth's position, a move that produced immediate dividends as the Quakers regained the lead on the hour mark. Elliott's pass found Himsworth running into the area and he pulled the ball back perfectly for Naylor to side-foot home.

The response from Forest was almost immediate, as only a minute later David Prutton had a header towards the bottom corner well saved by Van der Geest. Platt introduced himself from the bench and within ten minutes Forest were level again. Bart-Williams found Alan Rogers in space on the left and his left-footed drive took a deflection off Neil Aspin into the net past the helpless Van der Geest. Darlington almost snatched victory in the 83rd minute when Naylor cleverly opened up the Forest defence and set up Williamson, but his effort rolled agonisingly wide.

The Quakers had acquitted themselves well against a team from two divisions above and could be pleased with a 2-2 draw. Ian and I certainly shared that sentiment as he pushed me home.

NOTTINGHAM FOREST V DARLINGTON – LEAGUE CUP FIRST ROUND SECOND LEG 2000/01

I'd been to the City Ground once before to see Newcastle play. If my memory serves me right, Gary Megson scored for the Magpies in an entertaining 1-1 draw. This was a far better prospect though, as it was the first time I'd seen Darlo play there.

I made the journey with Ian straight from work in his car. We got into the ground just in time for the kick-off, having left Darlington at five o'clock. The two of us went into the disabled area to witness what was an enthralling game. Forest were two leagues above us but the way Darlington played that night you would never have thought it.

The home team had the better of the first half and scored in the 15th minute through Stern John. As a matter of interest, John was partnered up front by Robbie Blake, the former Darlington forward who was part of Darlington's Wembley squad in 1996. After the goal Darlington seemed to settle and I remember that winger Mark Angel was particularly impressive. He had a shot that was brilliantly saved by Dave Beasant.

Midway through the second half former youth team player Paul Campbell scored a tremendous goal from 20 yards to equalise. The Darlington fans, including Ian and I, went absolutely crazy. We were by this time well on top, and Stuart Elliott scored one of the best goals I have ever seen from a Darlo player. Beasant kicked the ball out, it landed at Elliott's feet and from fully 50 yards he lobbed it into the middle of the net to score what can only be described as a truly magnificent goal. Despite having to weather some heavy Forest pressure, Darlington held on for what was a memorable victory.

After the final whistle, George Reynolds embraced Gary Bennett in front of the Darlington fans as the players enjoyed their moment of victory. These were scenes I'll never forget.

BRADFORD CITY V DARLINGTON – LEAGUE CUP SECOND ROUND SECOND LEG 2000/01

Following the Nottingham Forest victory, Darlington were drawn against Premier League strugglers Bradford City in the second round. Ian, Ben and I travelled to that match, again in Ian's car.

I can remember thinking during our journey that we didn't have much hope of winning the tie as Gary Bennett, in his ultimate wisdom, had decided to rest several first-team players for the second leg. I thought this was a strange decision, especially as we had only lost the first leg 1-0 at Feethams, so there was still all to play for.

As with Nottingham Forest, we arrived at the ground just before kick-off; Ben accompanied me into the disabled area while Ian went into the away end.

The game was out of Darlo's reach as early as the ninth minute as Bradford were 3-0 up by then. Italian star striker Benito Carbone had our defence at sixes and sevens, scoring one and creating the other two. By half-time the score was 4-0 and Ben and I were ready to go home.

Early in the second half City scored their fifth goal and all of a sudden Darlington burst into life. Stuart Elliott and Mark Angel scored two quick-fire goals to make the score 5-2; however, before the end, Bradford added a further two to make the final score a very dispiriting 7-2.

I had been correct. Bennett's decision to play practically a reserve team had cost us dearly, and a far superior team had hammered us.

Anyway, let me just add a few words about Benito Carbone. He was absolutely brilliant that night, although he wasn't exactly playing against a team of superstars!

DARLINGTON V SHREWSBURY – 2000/01

Following the hammering at Bradford City, Darlo slid down the league and by February we were languishing in 20th position.

To add to the summer exoduses, both Neil Aspin and Lee Nogan left late in 2000, joining Hartlepool United and Luton Town respectively. Not finding adequate replacements for these two experienced players only compounded the problems in my opinion.

Nogan and Aspin were fairly high earners so to me it was no surprise when they left. Aspin, in particular, was a great miss due to his wealth of experience. While not a prolific goalscorer, Nogan was certainly a damn sight better than the forwards he left behind him following his departure, with the exception of Glenn Naylor.

So by the time we played Shrewsbury at home in April the fans were clearly frustrated and disappointed by the lack of progress that the team had made on the pitch especially after the success they had enjoyed the previous season. It was therefore not surprising when they started to get on George Reynolds's back and even barracked him prior to the kick-off.

In hindsight, he was putting all his spare cash into building the new stadium and hadn't set aside sufficient funds for team building. I personally disagreed with this policy. Wigan Athletic, for example, built a decent team first before moving into their new JJB Stadium. Dave Whelan, the Latics' owner at the time and himself a former player, did things the right way whereas George was building our new stadium – one that the fans didn't particularly want – at the team's expense.

Anyway, enough of my moaning and back to the Shrewsbury game. Darlington took the lead through left-back Olivier Bernard, on loan from Newcastle United, early in the first half. He scored after good work from the captain Craig Liddle who crossed well. Just before the half-hour, Mark Kilty scored after a brilliant run and cross from left-winger Richard Hodgson.

Ben and I were sitting together in the disabled area and simply couldn't believe it. However, things got even better just before half-time when the ever-reliable Naylor made it 3-0, again after good work by Hodgson. While having my half-time pint in Strikers I kept on saying to everyone that we were 3-0 up, still not quite believing it.

The second half was almost as good with recent acquisition Mark Convery, signed from Sunderland, and

Naylor going close to adding to our tally. But the game ended up with the scoreline of 3-0.

I was very impressed by the performances of Bernard, Convery, Naylor and Liddle; all four were magnificent throughout.

HARTLEPOOL UNITED V DARLINGTON – 2001/02

Following on from the previous campaign, I knew that 2001/02 was going to be one hard slog since, once again, many players who simply weren't good enough were representing the club.

One of the main reasons for this was the fact that George Reynolds had further tightened the purse strings due to spending ever-increasing amounts of cash on the half-built new stadium.

This in turn meant that Gary Bennett was unable to bring in players of a high-enough calibre to succeed.

Several squad members were released, including popular centre-forward Jesper Hjorth. Incomings included Neil Maddison, who actually was a good signing, Barry Conlon from York, and winger Neil Wainwright returned permanently following his successful loan spell two seasons previously. Unfortunately, the remainder of the signings simply weren't up to the job.

The season actually started brightly and included a 2-1 win over Hartlepool United, a game that I attended with Ben. The two of us went there on the train, arriving in Hartlepool at around one o'clock. With time to spare we visited the working men's club near the ground where we were made really welcome by the bar staff, and after consuming a couple of pints we headed to Victoria Park.

Just after we had got comfortable, Darlington went behind with Kevin Tinkler scoring following a corner. To their credit, despite losing Neil Maddison to injury, Darlington didn't simply crumble, and equalised through Brian Atkinson who slotted the ball home after good work by substitute Richard Hodgson. A few minutes later Ben and I were in dreamland as Gary Bennett's men took the lead through Danny Mellanby after being set up by the excellent Wainwright.

In the second half Darlington could and maybe should have increased their lead. One chance saw Richard Hodgson one on one with the Hartlepool keeper Martin Hollund. Unfortunately, his shot was blocked and the chance was gone. The home team did put the Darlington defence under pressure in the latter stages but we held on for a famous victory. The scenes after the match were brilliant with Bennett dancing with the players; this was a rare event as he very seldom showed his emotions. It was actually brilliant to witness.

SCUNTHORPE UNITED V DARLINGTON – LDV TROPHY FIRST ROUND 2001/02

Following the excellent win over Hartlepool, Darlo were sixth in the league but things started to go badly wrong and it came as no surprise to me when Gary Bennett resigned from his post in October 2001. I had always liked Bennett and thought he was unfortunate not to manage the club at a different time.

Bennett stayed on as reserve team manager and was replaced by former Cambridge United and Leyton Orient boss. I can remember thinking that whoever was in charge would continue to struggle unless the chairman loosened the purse strings. I turned out to be correct in my assumption.

Taylor's first official game in charge, following the dismal 1-0 defeat at home to Hull which Bennett's assistant manager Mick Tait took charge of, was away to Scunthorpe United in the LDV Trophy. Ian accompanied me to this game on the train.

The two of us left Darlington at midday, arriving in Doncaster at one o'clock. We therefore decided to go to The Railway for a few drinks before continuing our journey to Scunthorpe. We smirked when we noticed that clock behind the bar was still ten minutes slow!

Anyway, after a few hours we were on our travels again, this time catching a local train for the remainder of our journey. Once at our destination, we hailed a cab to take us to the Berkeley pub, where we had been on our previous visit.

Unlike 1989, the place was bereft of Darlington fans. After having something to eat we headed for the ground, in what was an absolutely freezing night.

To be honest, I thought on more than one occasion during the game that I'd rather be sitting at home in the warmth of my living room, listening on the radio, especially after witnessing what can only be described as a poor excuse for a match that night.

Taylor sprang a couple of surprises in what was his first team selection. Frank van der Geest made a rare appearance in goal and youth team striker Mark Sheeran was named among the substitutes. Unfortunately, inspirational captain Craig Liddle was out with a long-term injury. He was replaced by David Brightwell, and no disrespect to him, but it wasn't exactly a like for like swap.

Darlington actually started quite brightly, with Barry Conlon going the closest to scoring. Unfortunately, his strike partner Kirk Jackson, signed from non-league Worksop Town, looked way out of his depth, hence 'Bazza' was basically having to forage up front on his own, something he'd get used to during his Darlo career.

It came as no surprise as following a sustained period of pressure early in the second half the hosts took the lead through Lee Hodges. Former Darlo forward Martin Carruthers quickly added a second following good work by Peter Beagrie. After that, Darlo capitulated and it became a matter of how many the Iron would score. However, their fans had to be content with only one more goal, scored by Jamie McCombe, again after good work by man-of-the-match Beagrie.

Overall, it had been a horrendous second-half performance, with Van der Geest, Brightwell, Simon Betts and Jackson all particularly poor. If Taylor didn't know what he was letting himself in for prior to the game, he certainly did afterwards.

DARLINGTON V LEYTON ORIENT – (LAST EVER GAME AT FEETHAMS) 2002/03

On the first Saturday in May 2003, Darlington played their last competitive fixture at Feethams, against Leyton Orient, before embarking upon a new era at their not yet fully completed 27,500 all-seater stadium.

While being pushed through the gates by Ian, probably for the very last time, my mind wandered back to that cold, foggy January Saturday afternoon back in 1973, when my by now late mother had pushed me through those very same gates to witness the 7-0 defeat at the hands of Southport. That was where it had all started for me, a love affair with a football club that was still as strong in 2003 as it had been just over 30 years earlier. Had I been a sentimental sort of person I might well have shed a tear, but I'm not and so I didn't. However, I wondered instead what my mother would have thought if she'd been pushing me instead of Ian. I guess she'd have said something like, 'You have to move with the times, Paul.' I knew she would have been right but it still was a sad day for me, and it was, I know, the same for hundreds of other Darlo fans, not only based in Darlington, but all over the world.

As usual, the pair of us went to Strikers, meeting up with Ben for a quicker-than-normal pint as I wanted to see the parade of former players who had graced Feethams over the decades. These included record goalscorer Alan Walsh (now a scout at Stoke City), my all-time hero Kevan Smith, record appearance maker Ron Greener (now no longer with us), Jimmy Willis and the now sadly departed Paul Willis, as well as David Speedie, Dale Anderson, Ron Ferguson, my friend Mark Forster, David Corner, John Borthwick plus many, many others. It was a spectacle that would live on in my memory forever.

To me, and probably every other Darlo fan in the ground, the game was almost secondary, but Leyton Orient were not there just to make up the numbers and threatened to spoil the send-off by racing into a two-goal lead through Matthew Lockwood and Gary Alexander. However, Darlo fought back with a reply through Jim Corbett, on loan from Blackburn Rovers, almost on the stroke of half-time. It was then left to Neil Wainwright to restore parity with only quarter of an hour remaining, just a minute after having come on to the pitch as a replacement for Ryan Valentine. It was fitting that Neil became the last professional to score at Feethams as he was still a stalwart of the team until his eventual departure in 2008, though he did return to the club in their hour of need during the 2009/10 season.

At the final whistle, the pitch was deluged by masses of Darlo fans, some of them clutching souvenirs such as seat numbers, pieces of turf from the pitch or anything else they could lay their hands on, wanting to savour every remaining second of this unique occasion.

Everybody wanted to say goodbye to Feethams in their own private way. For my own part, I simply sat in the East Stand, with Ian only a few seats away, surrounded by many happy and some not so happy memories. While I was there daydreaming, several thoughts suddenly came back into my mind. Why did we have to move? Would the new ground end up being a noose around the club's neck, just like the East Stand had done during the ill-fated Mike Peden era?

These questions had been niggling away at me for months. They needed answering, but by whom? George Reynolds, perhaps? Although it was obvious that he wanted to build one of the most impressive grounds in the country, it was taking up far too much money, which could have been better spent on the team. Something simply wasn't right in my mind. Why not redevelop Feethams instead?

We had a magnificent East Stand that was less than five years old at the time. Surely the rest of the ground could have been brought up to the same standard? However, the decision had already been made and that was that. Nevertheless, I was still very uneasy about the whole situation.

My thoughts were interrupted when Ben appeared where Ian and I were sitting. The three of us then went for one last pint in Strikers. Strikers had always meant a lot to me.

DARLINGTON V KIDDERMINSTER HARRIERS – 2003/04

After saying goodbye to Feethams, Darlington played their first game at the newly built Reynolds Arena against Kidderminster Harriers.

However, it wasn't particularly the match that became the focus of the fans' attention so much as being able to experience the new stadium.

Ian and I, knowing that there would be a large crowd at the game, arrived at the stadium at about one o'clock on what was a searingly hot day. To our disbelief we couldn't even get into the bar for a drink because it was already full to overflowing.

After buying a programme and giving up any idea of obtaining a drink, we decided to enter the stadium and try our luck inside.

The pair of us were extremely disappointed when we found that the bar in the concourse didn't have a pump connected and the bottles and cans that were meant to be a substitute for the draught beers were not available until half-time.

By this time the queues outside the stadium were enormous and the kick-off had to be delayed for a good

15 minutes. The North Stand was still not fully finished and therefore could not be used. All in all, everything seemed rushed and ill-prepared.

Once inside, at pitch level we found that the seats were filthy. Before Ian sat down he had to wipe the plastic with some tissues, which wasn't good at all.

Little did we know, but the club had inadvertently hired a comedian to entertain the crowd. His name you may ask? None other than George Reynolds! When he came strutting on to the pitch, microphone in hand, for a quick second I thought it was Roy Chubby Brown. He then went on to make one of the most incredible speeches I have ever heard during his time at Darlington. First of all, he rounded on the 'Doubting Thomases' who he asked to stand up. Then he made the claim that with one or two new players we would become an unstoppable force on our way to the Premier League. After hearing such nonsense, I thought that maybe he'd been out too long in the midday sun and was suffering from a case of sunstroke.

Speaking of sunstroke, the concourse bar did eventually open but the queues were absolutely horrendous. People were pushing each other in a vain attempt to get a drink and Ian was almost knocked flying by a man who was trying to get served.

Eventually he returned with *one* bottle of water, which we shared. We were both really dehydrated by this time and the water wasn't enough but it was all Ian could obtain. Several fans were close to passing out due to the heat, yet there was nothing the stewards could do for them. The whole thing was a complete farce.

After looking at the team, I thought that we needed eight or nine new players rather than the 'one or two' that Reynolds had mentioned.

In my opinion, manager Mick Tait, who had replaced Tommy Taylor the previous season, had built a team with not only his hands tied behind his back but his legs chopped off as well.

An example of this was bringing in players such as Glen Robson and Fabien Bossy who were not even Conference standard. In addition to this, several former youth team players made up the numbers. These included Chris Hughes, David McGurk and Mark Sheeran, all of whom were good players, but not good enough to play league football week in week out at that particular time. The reason for this was that they needed to mature and progress, rather than be chucked in and be expected to become regular first-team players. Most of the money had continued to be spent on the new stadium rather than on the team, which simply wasn't right.

The team that took the field against Kidderminster Harriers, in my opinion, was on paper one of the worst I had seen since the 1970s and it came as no surprise that they performed abominably and lost 2-0 with goals from Danny Williams and Andy Bishop.

A lot of the 11,600 supporters who had attended the match had seen the new era go flat on the very first day.

Many of them would never return. The club had blown the chance to gain new fans through being ill-prepared for the big day and, far more importantly, having a very poor team to boot.

HORNCHURCH V DARLINGTON – FA CUP FIRST ROUND 2003/04

Apart from September when they actually went on an unbeaten run, Darlo struggled in 2003/04. After a disastrous October, David Hodgson replaced the unfortunate Mick Tait and took over for what was his third and final stint as manager. Tait must have had one of the lowest budgets in the whole league. I have to admit, I felt really sorry for him as he had been on a hiding to nothing right from the day he had first accepted the job. To me, the appointment of Hodgson represented a last throw of the dice by a now desperate George Reynolds.

Reynolds must have swallowed his pride big time to bring the likeable Hodgson back in. In some ways I admired him for it. Hodgson is a good manager to have when the chips are down, which they were. But I still wasn't sure whether he'd be able to work with Reynolds. Things were made easier for Hodgson as part of the deal to bring him back was that Reynolds stayed away from the stadium. According to Hodgson, the reason for this was because the fans were on Reynolds's back and he wanted the focus to be on the team rather than the chairman. Thinking about this now, Hodgson's idea made perfect sense.

Hodgson's first official game in charge was away at non-league Hornchurch (many years later, he informed me that midfielder Martin Gray had in fact picked the team) in the FA Cup first round, a game that I again attended with Ian. With it being a Sunday fixture, the two of us travelled on the Saturday before the game, staying in a hotel overnight.

We set off early on the Sunday morning to the ground and headed straight to the bar where fellow Darlo fans John Gray and Richard Jones met us; both were confident of an easy win. The way we'd been playing, though, I wasn't so sure.

A quick word about the ground itself. I have to say, it was actually one of the better non-league ones I'd visited up until that time. The bar was roomy and the people very welcoming.

Anyway, about 15 minutes before kick-off we took our places in the away end. Darlo started brightly and almost scored when midfielder Ashley Nicholls curled a shot narrowly wide after good work by Clark Keltie. We continued to push forward, but in the 43rd minute Keltie brought down a Hornchurch player in the box. He needn't have done so as the fouled player was heading away from goal. Anyway, forward Steve West gleefully rammed home the resulting penalty to give the hosts the lead at the interval.

I soon noticed during the second half that some of the Darlo players didn't seem to have the heart for the fight. This annoyed me as Ian and I had spent well in excess of £300 each in train fares, hotel bills, taxi fares, entrance money, food and drinks. The least we could expect was that the team would show some battling spirit. Unfortunately, they just lay down and died.

It came as no surprise to the pair of us when the non-leaguers doubled their lead in the 61st minute through Vinnie Johns who tapped in from six yards following a cross that took out the whole of the Darlo back four as well as hapless goalkeeper Michael Price. As far as I was concerned, the game was dead, and I was right. We ended up being beaten by a team two leagues below us. I was seething after witnessing such a gutless display, as was Ian.

BILLINGHAM SYNTHONIA V DARLINGTON – 2007/08

I made the short journey with Ian in his car to see Billingham Synthonia take on Darlo in a pre-season friendly.

Despite the journey being short, we still took the wrong turning off the A19. This was my fault as I thought I knew a 'quicker' route but ended up (much to Ian's amusement) leading us totally the wrong way. So much for my sense of direction. Anyway, Ian quickly turned the car around and we were at the ground in no time. 'No harm done,' I blurted out. Well, I would say that wouldn't I!

On entering the ground the three of us headed for the bar for a quick pint before kick-off. John Gray and Richard Jones were already in there, along with several other Darlo fans. Richard said that the pair of them left Darlington by train, arrived at Thornaby only to find that their connection had been cancelled. With this in mind, they headed to Stockton, consumed a few pints there before catching a train to Billingham. 'Quite an adventure for a friendly,' I thought. Luckily for them, another Darlo fan offered them a lift back after the match, which was a decent gesture.

With five minutes to go before kick-off we left the bar and went to watch the match. Darlo fielded a very strong team, mostly comprising first-team players.

While watching the game, Ian and I were joined by Darlington's youth development officer at that particular time, Mick Tait. I had known Mick for many years. He had been a player in the early 1990s before becoming manager, and I had always got on really well with him. He seemed to be really optimistic for the new season, which was good to hear.

Anyway, back to the game in question. Darlo took the lead through new signing Ian Harty's fourth goal during pre-season, following an excellent run and cross from Julian Joachim. Unfortunately, Neil Wainwright took a bad knock during the first half and this to me definitely affected his game. Substitute Gregg Blundell added a second, again following good work by Joachim, who for the second time in the game produced a good cross from the right to set up the goal. Shortly after that goal, both sides brought on several subs which disrupted the flow of the game and Darlo seemed content to see it out, eventually winning 2-0.

Personally, I'd have liked to have seen a few more goals, but on the positive side Harty and Joachim stood out – in addition the defence looked solid. One word about Billingham Synthonia. I thought their keeper, John Jackson, who started his career at Middlesbrough, was outstanding. He made several excellent saves and I left the ground wondering why he wasn't at a Football League club.

BARNSLEY V DARLINGTON – LEAGUE CUP FIRST ROUND 2007/08

In August 2007, I made the fairly short journey to Barnsley for our League Cup tie, with Ian and John Gray in Ian's car.

During our trip my mind began to wander and I began to think about former players who Darlo had signed from Barnsley over the years. The two who sprung to mind were David Speedie and Carl Airey. Over the years I have kept in contact with David. One thing about him is if I have ever needed any help with charity events, he has always assisted, which is great.

Looking back, I really think that Airey was one of the main reasons why we were so successful in winning promotion in 1984/85. After leaving Darlo in 1986 he had a spell in Belgium before returning to England to play for Chesterfield and Torquay United. It was in Torquay during the early 1990s that Ian and I bumped into Carl in a pub – by then he had finished playing football and was a milkman. I always liked him and remember being gutted when he left the club. Without doubt, I'm of the opinion that both players would figure in Darlo's top 20 during my lifetime.

Anyway, in what seemed like no time we were at Oakwell. After parking up we headed to the Metrodome Leisure Complex near the ground for a couple of pints. While in there, I bumped into John Sotnik, Darlo's chief executive, who was having a coffee with former referee Jeff Winter and football club director Barrie Simmonds. Our main topic of conversation was my film and my recent trip to Cannes for the film festival. While I hadn't met Barrie before, I had previously had the pleasure of meeting Jeff at a sportsman's dinner two years previously at which he was the guest speaker. He was quite a funny guy that evening and had a lot to say for himself. On this occasion, however, he didn't have much to talk about, which I thought was unusual, apart from saying, 'Hello.' I don't think he remembered me to be honest.

Prior to leaving Darlington, I had arranged with our winger Neil Wainwright to obtain a couple of complimentary tickets for me and he dutifully had left them at the Oakwell reception area where Ian and I picked them up. I don't like hanging around at the players' entrance for free tickets, but if I can organise to have them left for me to pick up then I feel all right about it. The reason for this is that I hate to feel like a beggar, but each to their own, I suppose. After leaving the reception, Ian and I headed to the away disabled area to watch the game. John left us to join the rest of the Darlo fans in the seats.

The Quakers started brightly with Pawel Abbott going close to scoring after an excellent cross from Chris Palmer. Abbott only just failed to make contact with the ball and, if he had done so, it would have been a certain goal. Shortly after that, Stephen Foster almost scored with a header, again after good work by Palmer. Barnsley also had a couple of chances but David Stockdale looked solid in the Darlo goal. It was no surprise to both Ian and I that the game was goalless at the interval.

The second half started in much the same vein as the first with Palmer still in the thick of things. He had a deflected free kick that fell just short of Abbott who would have surely scored had he made contact. Barnsley took the lead shortly after through István Ferenczi following good work by Robert Kozluk, who set up the goal with an excellent cross. This seemed to spur Darlington on, and they equalised in the 70th minute through former Barnsley forward Tommy Wright, who volleyed the ball high into the net after full-back Rob Purdie had supplied the cross. Extra time seemed to be looming when Barnsley defender Paul Reid prodded the ball past Stockdale from around six yards out for what turned out to be the winning goal.

Despite losing the game 2-1, Ian, John and I agreed that Darlo had matched a side that were two divisions above us and that we had been unlucky not to at least force extra time.

Personally, despite being disappointed at losing, I'd rather win league games. After all, Darlo were never going to win the League Cup were they? With that thought in my mind, once Ian had got me into the car, I was quickly asleep and the next thing I knew we were back in Darlington dropping John off.

WREXHAM V DARLINGTON – 2007/08

The 2007/08 season brought an upturn in Darlington's fortunes. Former Doncaster Rovers manager Dave Penney was now in charge and he'd built a decent team that was challenging for promotion. George Reynolds had left the club, after putting it into administration, and the Sterling Consortium, whom George had owed money to, took control. Eventually they sold it to north-east businessman George Houghton, who was the owner at the start of this particular season.

A game that springs to mind was Wrexham away, which I went to with Ian on the train. Let me explain.

When I worked for the *Darlington Advertiser* in the early 1990s, I used to interview Brian Little on a regular basis.

During those interviews I always noticed that if he was confident that his team would win, he would have a glint in his eyes. Well, to my horror, he had exactly the same glint as I was talking to him in his office at the Racecourse Ground. He said that although Darlo had a good team, he was confident that his Wrexham side, who were in the bottom four at the time, would beat us, as he had done his homework.

After talking to Brian, I just knew we'd lose. Despite this, it was great to catch up with him again. As a footnote, I thought it was really kind of him to ask me to spend time with him pre-match.

That said, I'd always got on really well with him (and still do to this day), so it came as no surprise to me when he did this.

As things turned out, Brian turned out to be absolutely right as we witnessed Darlo's worst performance of the season.

After we left the stadium, Ian and I went to the Turf Hotel where we chatted with some Wrexham fans. They said that they thought Darlo were poor on the day and that Wrexham deserved the 2-0 win.

In all honesty I couldn't argue with those sentiments, which stuck in my mind during our long journey back to Darlington.

DARLINGTON V ROCHDALE – PLAY-OFF SEMI-FINAL FIRST LEG – 2007/08

Darlington finished fifth in the league that season and qualified for the play-offs where we played Rochdale, with the first leg of the semi-final at The Arena. I attended with Ann, my PA.

The match was broadcast live on Sky and I wondered if many fans would stay away and watch in the pub. I needn't have worried as a crowd of 8,057, the biggest of the season by far, was in the stadium to watch the match.

The two of us witnessed a brilliant Darlo performance, one that had us on the edge of our seats.

Darlington midfielder Jason Kennedy scored one of the best goals ever seen at The Arena in the first half. He received the ball from Leeds United loanee Ben Parker, and beat his man before curling it around the Rochdale keeper Tommy Lee and into the net. It was truly a brilliant goal, one that I wouldn't forget in a hurry. Minutes later, Alan White headed the ball wide following a good run and cross from Rob Purdie. The game continued to ebb and flow and Darlo were excellent value for their lead at the interval.

The Quakers were made to pay for several missed second-half opportunities when the visitors equalised in the 70th minute. Chris Dagnall got the ball on the Darlo left, shot from 25 yards, and unfortunately it struck Stephen Foster on his thigh before ending up in the back of the net. Darlo, to their credit, didn't let their heads drop and took the lead in the second minute of injury time. Neil Wainwright swung in a free kick from the left, and fellow substitute Ian Miller outjumped everyone to plant a header firmly past Tommy Lee. The home fans, including Ann and I, went wild. Shortly after the goal the final whistle went, which meant that Darlo had secured a slender lead to take to Spotland for the second leg.

ROCHDALE V DARLINGTON – PLAY-OFF SEMI-FINAL SECOND LEG – 2007/08

I was gutted that I wouldn't be able to attend the second leg as, for the second time, we'd be at the Cannes Film Festival promoting our film, *Give Them Wings*. At least we'd be able to watch it on the television though.

Ian, Ann, Andy Isaac (our film producer at the time) and I watched the match in an Irish bar called The Quays, in the centre of Cannes.

I'd had a few pints the night before so ordered a half pint of milk to settle my stomach. The barmaid found this highly amusing and took great delight in taking the mickey, as did Ann, Andy and Ian.

Darlo, with Neil Wainwright restored to the starting line-up, took the lead with what can only be described as a 'dodgy penalty' after 27 minutes. Clark Keltie crossed from the right, Rochdale striker Rene Howe challenged Jason Kennedy, and I have to say that in my opinion he hardly touched him. To our utter amazement the referee pointed to the spot. Keltie accepted his early Christmas present by blasting the ball into the back of the net. The goal put Darlo 3-1 up overall and seemingly in control of proceedings. However, Rochdale dispelled that myth and forced their way back into the game in the 43rd minute. Former Darlington winger Adam Rundle crossed from the left and Chris Dagnall forced the ball home from close range. 'Game on,' I thought.

During the break, I was confident that we'd hold on, and win the tie in the process; Ian, Ann and Andy weren't as sure. Ian and Ann were a bag of nerves, and for once I was chilled. Perhaps it was the milk.

Shortly after the restart, Keltie almost restored Darlo's two-goal lead but his 25-yard blockbuster hit the bar and rebounded to safety. Rochdale slowly took control of the game and levelled the tie in the 78th minute when David Perkins hit a shot from around 20 yards which looked to be going well wide until the ball hit Kennedy and flew past the helpless David Stockdale. My heart sank when the goal went in, and for the first time in the tie I had a feeling that Darlo were going to lose. Rochdale poured men forward at every opportunity and looked threatening on more than one occasion. With this in mind, I was more than happy to hear the final whistle with the overall scores level at 3-3. This meant extra time.

With there being so much at stake, both sides seemed nervous and created few chances. Rochdale were reduced to ten men in the 109th minute when Perkins was sent off for a cynical foul on Ricky Ravenhill. Following the dismissal, the home side seemed content to defend in numbers and play the game out, which they did with surprising ease. With the scores still level after extra time the match went to penalties.

Ann, Ian and I could hardly look as Guylain Ndumbu-Nsungu, Purdie, Wainwright and Ravenhill all put their penalties away, as did Dagnall, Tom Kennedy, Adam Le Fondre and Gary Jones for Rochdale. Jason Kennedy took Darlo's fifth kick and got it on target but Lee saved it. Former Manchester United winger Ben Muirhead stepped up to take Rochdale's final penalty, blasting the ball past Stockdale to send his team to Wembley.

We were all absolutely gutted. All credit to Rochdale but we would have beaten them with a full-strength side, of that I have no doubt.

DARLINGTON V ROCHDALE – 2008/09

I went to almost every game, home and away during the 2008/09 season, until disaster struck. Let me explain.

For months there were rumours going about that the club, once again, were struggling for cash; chairman George Houghton, who had already slashed the playing budget at the end of the previous season, pleaded in the press for more fans to attend matches. Those appeals weren't answered and it came as no surprise to Ben, Ian and I when he placed the club into administration for the second time in its history.

I have to say, I was never really sure about Houghton as a chairman. Like George Reynolds before him, he led the fans up the garden path about funding. However, this wasn't the only reason – he came to the club full of promises and then pulled the rug from under manager Dave Penney's feet where promotion was concerned, as the club was immediately docked ten points for entering administration. This killed off any hopes of even reaching the play-offs.

I can remember the night Darlington went into administration as if it were yesterday. We were at home to Rochdale, and as Ian and I entered the stadium there were rumours going around regarding the club's financial position. This was even more apparent as we entered the bar.

Looking back now, that night signalled the beginning of the end for the club as I knew it, though I didn't realise it at the time.

The game itself was played out in a sombre atmosphere and Darlo lost 2-1, with midfielder Robin Hulbert scoring our goal.

With Darlington entering administration, all the loanees left and returned to their clubs, leaving a frustrated Penney with a threadbare squad that couldn't really compete. They dropped down the league as a consequence.

CHESTER CITY V DARLINGTON – 2008/09

By the time Darlo played their last league game of the season at Chester City, Dave Penney had quit to go and manage Oldham Athletic, and his assistant Martin Gray was in charge of team affairs.

Ian and I made the trip to the Deva Stadium, not really knowing whether it could be our last ever fixture.

As the pair of us entered the bar, some Darlo fans were close to tears and in a state of shock at what had gone on. Personally I wasn't as I'd seen it all before; yes, I was disappointed with what had happened, but the club had overspent and this was the result.

Once inside the ground, Ian and I witnessed a spirited performance from Darlo which saw them eventually win 2-1 with both goals scored by Pawel Abbott – the winner coming in what was almost the last kick of the match.

After the game had ended, the players came out and threw their shirts into the crowd. Ian and I both knew that most of them wouldn't be at the club the following season, heralding yet another downturn in fortunes.

GRIMSBY TOWN V DARLINGTON – 2009/10

The 2008/09 season ended with Darlington still in administration. All but three of the professional players had left the club by the start of the 2009/10 season. Those three loyal players deserve to be mentioned. They were captain Stephen Foster, fellow centre-half Ian Miller, and goalkeeper Nick Liversedge. These were joined by four former youth team players: Curtis Main, Josh Gray, Dan Groves and Dan Riley.

George Houghton's former business partner Raj Singh bought the club and took it out of administration. On the downside, Darlington no longer owned The Arena as the former chairman had bought it with 'borrowed' money and the businessmen who hadn't been repaid took up ownership of the stadium instead. This meant the club was back to paying rent to a landlord, an absolute disgrace in my opinion.

Anyway, former Middlesbrough boss Colin Todd was brought in as the new team manager, and he wasted no time in bringing in ten new players.

Unfortunately, to a man, they were all substandard and following our first game of the season, a 3-1 defeat at Aldershot Town (loanee David Dowson getting the Darlo goal), a game I attended with Ian, we knew we were on a hiding to nothing and would struggle to stay up. The team was simply awful on that summer's day.

By the time Ian and I went to the Grimsby away match in September 2009, we were rooted to the foot of the table and the gossip around the ground was that Todd was going to be sacked. The team actually played well that day and managed to earn a creditable 1-1 draw with substitute Main getting the goal. The gossip Ian and I had heard earlier was correct and Todd was sacked after the match.

TORQUAY UNITED V DARLINGTON –
2009/10

Colin Todd was replaced by former Republic of Ireland boss Steve Staunton. Looking back, this was probably Raj Singh's worst footballing decision of his ill-fated tenure.

All Staunton did was bring in what can only be described as poor players from Ireland, and that's being kind. The majority of them weren't even Northern League standard. Paddy Dean in particular springs to mind; he must be the worst player to don an outfield shirt in the 50 years I have supported the club.

The team were getting hammered most weeks; Ian and I couldn't believe what we were seeing.

Torquay United away in December 2009 sticks in my mind to this day. I made the long journey for this fixture with Ian in his car.

The pair of us witnessed a 5-0 mauling, together with what is still one of the most inept Darlington performances I have seen to this day. There didn't appear to be any fight at all and the small contingent of fans who had made the considerable effort to get to Plainmoor, at great expense, were understandably very angry at the final whistle.

The two of us waited for Staunton at the players' entrance after the match, as did several other fans who had made the 600-mile round trip. He didn't even have the decency to speak to us. The supporters were fuming and the players came in for a lot of stick, simply because the manager wouldn't face the fans. He headed for the sanctuary of the team bus and put his head down, leaving his players to face the flak instead of him. I thought this was an act of cowardice and therefore was wrong, and showed he had no real affiliation to either the club or indeed its fans.

By March 2010, even Singh had seen enough and with the team as good as down he fired Staunton, not before time in my opinion.

The hapless Staunton was replaced by former Darlo loanee Simon Davey. Results improved slightly, but the damage had already been done and we were relegated to the Conference National.

I was gutted, but not at all surprised. Singh had made too many mistakes and it cost us our Football League status, simple as.

The club was again rocked during the close season when Davey walked out and took over at Hereford United. Davey's assistant Ryan Kidd was appointed but resigned after only a few days. It could only happen at Darlo.

Former Hartlepool United player Mark Cooper was then appointed in time for the start of the 2010/11 season.

5

The 2010s

MANSFIELD TOWN V DARLINGTON – FA TROPHY FINAL AT WEMBLEY 2010/11

I first met our new manager after the first game of the 2010/11 season, a 1-0 win over Newport at The Arena (Liam Hatch got the goal). I have to say that my first impressions of him weren't good at all.

Mark Cooper appeared in the bar post-match, sat at our table and proceeded to slate a couple of his players, who shall remain nameless. 'How unprofessional,' I thought. I'd have never seen Cyril Knowles, Brian Little, David Hodgson or Dave Penney behave like that. To me, he should have said what he said in the dressing room, not in the bar where all and sundry could hear. It's something that I never forgot and simply couldn't get my head around.

Despite my ongoing doubts about our manager, it didn't stop me from supporting the team and I still went to almost every game that season and to my amazement we got to Wembley in the FA Trophy. We'd finished in the top half of the league as well. Progress, so I thought.

I made the trip to London with Ann, along with around 10,000 other Darlo fans. The two of us travelled to the capital by train on the day of the match. Once there, we met up with Ian and Stephen.

After a few pints in The Green Man, the four of us headed for the stadium. Ann and I went to our place in the disabled area in plenty of time for the kick-off, leaving Stephen and Ian to finish their drinks, purchased in the concourse.

The pair of us witnessed a brilliant match. There were chances at both ends, although it was goalless at full time and the game went into extra time.

In the very last seconds Tommy Wright hit the bar; the rebound fell to fellow striker Chris Senior who headed the ball home. The Darlo fans, including Ann and I, went absolutely crazy. Within seconds of the restart the referee blew for time, and Darlo had won the FA Trophy.

It was absolutely brilliant to see the ever-loyal Ian Miller pick up the trophy; if anyone deserved that, it was him.

I'll never forget that day. It's firmly etched in my mind along with Crewe in 1984/85, Welling in 1989/90, and Wembley 1995/96 and 1999/2000.

BARROW V DARLINGTON – 2011/12

I actually went into the 2011/12 season feeling fairly optimistic; how wrong I was. The heart of the FA Trophy-winning team, including match-winner Chris Senior, had been released during the summer by Mark Cooper. Interestingly, both of the players he'd slated during our very first meeting were also released. This was a huge mistake on his part in my opinion.

At the time, all the team needed was a couple of new players, just like in 2000/01. If they had been signed, and others kept, I have no doubt that we would have been fighting at the top end of the league. However, this never happened, and eventually contributed to the disaster that was to follow.

Money was in short supply and in October 2011 Cooper was sacked, following a run of poor results, with youth team coach and former club captain Craig Liddle taking over. Shortly after that, Raj Singh put Darlington into their third spell of administration. I have to say, despite Cooper winning the FA Trophy for the club, I never took to him as a manager. Maybe first impressions do last.

We arranged for our then film director Dan Perry to take some footage of Ian's and my trip to the Barrow game, which many thought would be our last ever match. It was used to make a promo trailer which looked really good, to be fair. Ian, Dan and I made the journey to Cumbria in Ian's car.

Once we were there, the three of us noticed the tense atmosphere. This was particularly apparent when almost 500 Darlo fans applauded the team as they got off the bus. We filmed this and it's actually very moving to watch, even now, ten years later.

The occasion got to a lot of the Darlington players and they were soundly beaten 3-0 with Barrow's goals coming from Adam Boyes and two for Andy Cook.

After the match, the three of us stayed behind and shot some more footage. But both Ian and I thought that it was the end for our beloved club.

The Barrow match turned out to be the last appearance for most of the senior players, even Ian Miller left to join Grimsby. One could hardly blame him. He'd been through this before, maybe he thought, *'Enough is enough.'*

In the intervening weeks, Ben, Ian and I under the banner of our then film company, PIMM Productions Limited, donated several hundred pounds to the club, along with many other fans. This kept the club going until the end of the season. Long-serving fans Doug Embleton and Shaun Campbell deserve a special mention for the effort they put in by securing the necessary funds. I have known Doug for many years, and we served on the supporters' trust board together. He's a man who I hugely respect for the way he does things – i.e. the correct way.

Anyway, back to what I was saying. Unfortunately, Craig Liddle had to make do with mostly youth team players despite Neil Wainwright's emotional return to the club. Sadly, despite his presence, we lost almost every game and ended up in the relegation zone.

Unfortunately, due to all the creditors not being paid, the club was punished by the FA and relegated five divisions to the Northern League. In addition, the old company was closed and the club renamed Darlington 1883. To this day, I feel that we had been extremely harshly treated. I did consider not going again, but something pulled me back. Maybe it was the memories I'd made over the years, I don't know.

BISHOP AUCKLAND V DARLINGTON – 2012/13

Darlington started off the 2012/13 season in the Northern League, with a whole new squad, including several former players and a new manager in former player and youth team coach Martin Gray.

Although the game against Bishop Auckland was away, Darlington were ground-sharing with our hosts that day as we couldn't play at The Arena following our relegation.

Despite still being raw from the happenings of the previous season, I still made the short trip to Heritage Park with Ian in his car.

We were both pleasantly surprised by what we saw at our new temporary home. There was a bar upstairs, which was no problem as a lift was on site to provide access. The good thing about this was that if it was raining, I could watch the game from inside. I thought this was great, especially as there wasn't a lot of cover in the ground.

The two of us witnessed an entertaining match with Bishop Auckland taking the lead in the 47th minute through Andrew Johnson. This seemed to wake Darlington up and we certainly stepped up a gear. Goals from Arjun Purewal and returning Quakers Sean Reay and David Dowson gave Darlington their first win of their Northern League campaign.

Although I was pleased with the win, I thought the experience was surreal. Playing at such a low level was certainly different!

DARLINGTON V TEAM NORTHUMBRIA – 2012/13

Darlington continued their Northern League campaign by winning most of their matches, albeit there were blips along the way, notably defeats at Guisborough Town, Newton Aycliffe and away at Team Northumbria. However, on their day, the Quakers were simply far too strong for most of their rivals.

I went to the Team Northumbria match at Heritage Park with Ian, knowing that if Darlington won they'd clinch promotion to the Northern Premier League Division One North.

The ground was packed to the rafters and Darlington missed loads of gilt-edged chances before eventually going behind just ahead of half-time. However, the goal appeared to make the home side play with more of a sense of urgency and they equalised shortly after through a well-taken goal scored by former Middlesbrough winger Chris Emms. It was certainly a relief to have my pint up in the bar during the interval knowing that we were on level terms with our visitors, especially after witnessing them beat us earlier in the season.

Darlington started the second half very much in the same way as they had ended the first. It came as no surprise when striker Amar Purewell brilliantly headed home following an excellent run and cross from right-back Stephen Harrison. Darlo continued to dominate the match but were denied by a mixture of good goalkeeping and poor finishing by their forwards. However, they weren't to be denied forever and Amar Purewell made sure of the victory in injury time after running on to a through ball from Kerry Hedley (if memory serves me right), and slotting past the visiting keeper. A few seconds later, the final whistle went which meant Darlington had completed the first step on their long journey back up the football pyramid by clinching promotion and winning the Northern League title.

The scenes post-match were brilliant with manager Martin Gray celebrating with both his players and indeed the fans.

After watching the celebrations, Ian and I left the ground happy in the knowledge that we had clinched promotion, but knowing that there would probably be stiffer challenges ahead the following season.

DARLINGTON V BAMBER BRIDGE – NORTHERN PREMIER LEAGUE DIVISION ONE NORTH PLAY-OFF FINAL – 2014/15

Ian and I were correct with our assertion that life would be tougher in the Northern Premier League Division One North.

Darlington did, however, qualify for the play-offs in 2013/14 but were beaten 2-0 by Ramsbottom United at Heritage Park, meaning that our quest to climb up the leagues was halted by one season.

The following season Darlington finished second in the league and again qualified for the play-offs. After beating local rivals Spennymoor Town over two legs, we played Bamber Bridge in the final at Heritage Park, a game I again went to with Ian in his car.

Just like the Team Northumbria match, the ground was packed with fans all hoping that we would have better luck than we had the previous season.

Bamber Bridge started the brighter of the two teams, and if it wasn't for Darlington defender Gary Brown clearing a goalbound effort off the line and goalkeeper Mark Bell making a brilliant save, we could have and maybe should have been 2-0 down. However, striker Nathan Cartman almost gave the Quakers the lead in the 20th minute when he brought a brilliant save from visiting keeper Lee Dovey with an excellent overhead kick. From the resulting corner, defender Terry Galbraith headed wide with the goal at his mercy. At this stage, the game could have gone either way.

The second half started with Darlington on the attack with Galbraith again heading wide from a corner by winger Adam Mitchell. It came as no surprise when Cartman scored after defender Alan White had flicked on a long throw from fellow defender Brown. Ian and I went absolutely wild from our vantage point. A few minutes later, striker Graeme Armstrong made it 2-0 to Darlington following an excellent free kick from Galbraith. Barring disaster, we were heading to the Northern Premier League Premier Division.

Shortly after the goal, Cartman hit the bar from well outside the box. However, the ball rebounded to Stephen Thompson, who blasted it wide. White then forced Dovey into a very good save when he shot from just inside the penalty area.

At this stage, Ian and I were wondering how many goals we were going to score. But the game settled down, until the last minute when Dovey was sent off for the visitors after he cleaned out Armstrong on the edge of the box. Ian and I agreed that the referee was left with no option. An outfield player went in goal, but he wasn't really tested as the referee blew his whistle for full time shortly afterwards.

For the second time in three seasons, Ian and I witnessed Martin Gray and the players celebrating with the fans. Personally, I was looking forward to our players pitting their wits against higher league opposition.

WHITBY TOWN V DARLINGTON – 2015/16

Darlington took to the Northern Premier League Premier Division like a duck to water and were in the top two or three positions throughout most of the 2015/16 season. By the time the Quakers played Whitby Town in April 2016, they needed a point to secure the championship and, with that, promotion to the National League North.

Unfortunately, due to serious health issues caused by a car accident, I couldn't attend the game, but here is what the *Northern Echo*'s Craig Stoddart said about that amazing night:

'Historically, Darlington do not do things easily, yet last night they clinched the championship in stunning style, winning 7-1 at Whitby Town.

'A draw would effectively have been enough to finish first ahead of Blyth Spartans, but Quakers left no room for doubt by sweeping aside the shell-shocked opposition.

'It was 5-0 after only 20 minutes, Graeme Armstrong scoring a ten-minute hat-trick as Darlington put on a show for the thousands of their fans who enjoyed a party atmosphere at the Turnbull Ground.

'They were serenading their team as "champions" long before the break having made sure of victory and the club's third promotion in four seasons on a truly special night.

'It means Darlington will be in the National League North next season, the division they would have been in had the Football Association not demoted them to the Northern League four years ago.

'The trauma of that year now feels a world away for Quakers, however, who are now on 104 points, Blyth on 99 with one game to play.

'Blyth have pushed them all the way, but an astonishing run of 14 wins in 15 games has seen Martin Gray's men clinch the championship, with last night's win the most emphatic of the lot.

'Stephen Thompson got the first after three minutes, rounding the Town keeper after Armstrong's flick-on. Arguably the team's most important goal of the season was their 100th this season, and soon they had a 101st with Kevin Burgess on target yet again. Playing against the club he spent nine years with before moving to Quakers last summer, the centre-back headed home his 11th goal of the season after meeting a Terry Galbraith corner.

Then Armstrong took over. Adam Mitchell, who had replaced the suspended Chris Hunter at right-back, swung over a cross for Armstrong to thump home a bullet header for 3-0.

'At this stage only ten minutes had been played and Darlington supporters were almost as stunned as Whitby's players.

'Blyth had been hoping for a Town win to keep their title hopes alive, but Quakers were simply a class above, several classes in fact. So dominant were they that goalkeeper Peter Jameson did not touch the ball for the first 15 minutes, and his team-mates added a fourth goal on 17 minutes. Midfielder Leon Scott dribbled beyond a defender on the right and crossed for Armstrong to convert.

'Nathan Cartman, desperate to join in the fun, saw a header go just over, leading to keeper Shane Bland going ballistic with his defenders, but he was soon picking the ball out of his net again when it was 5-0. This time Armstrong stooped to head home against his former club from a Mitchell corner, the celebrations among the players almost muted by this stage so used were they to scoring. Darlington were going up in style, their proud supporters never having experienced anything like this, more used to going through the mill when seeing their team enjoy success.

'Since winning on the final day at Welling in 1990 to clinch promotion from the Conference, Quakers' fate is never usually settled until the final couple of games. Twelve months after Welling they also won the Division Four title on the last day against Rochdale, the Northern League in 2012/13 was not secured until their penultimate match, despite a record-breaking points total, and a year ago it was through the play-offs promotion was achieved. Even when promotion was not at stake, at Wembley in 2011, Quakers only overcame Mansfield Town thanks to a goal in the dying seconds of extra time, so last night's landslide was a welcome surprise for hardened Darlington fans.

'An Armstrong diving header went over from a Mitchell cross, leading to a period of respite for poor Whitby, giving Darlington supporters time to digest what they were watching.

'Whitby even won a penalty after Gary Brown bundled over Michael Roberts. However, Jameson, celebrating his 23rd birthday, saved Roberts' spot kick. It was that sort of night. Terry Galbraith showed Roberts how it should be done, making it 6-0 with a penalty six minutes before the break after Callum Martin pushed Scott.

'The second half, naturally, was less eventful, Whitby seeing a bit more of Jameson's goal. David McTiernan, a former target of Gray, was narrowly off target with a first-time shot when meeting a corner. Dale Hopson, a former Darlington midfielder and on target when the teams drew 2-2 earlier in the season, tried a long-range effort that was inches over Jameson's bar.

'"We want Whitey on," sang the Darlington fans, desperate to see local hero Alan White make a 201st appearance for his hometown club. They had to wait a while before he came on, until after Scott added the seventh. He netted with a well-struck blast from inside the penalty area, and then entered White to a huge cheer from the Darlington fans, many of them filling the stand behind the dugouts where Gray struggled to make himself heard above the din. From a left-wing cross, Hopson headed home a Whitby goal, nothing more than a footnote on an occasion which belonged to the champions.

'Whitby made a plea on the public address system, saying to Quakers fans, "Please do not go on to the pitch. Please. How I'm going to stop you I don't know, but please do not go on the pitch." There was never a chance of his pleas being heard as Darlington's euphoric fans celebrated the title.'

I was over the moon that we had clinched promotion, for the second season in a row. However, I was gutted that I couldn't go to witness this brilliant Darlington performance. I was there in spirit though.

WALSALL V DARLINGTON – FA CUP FIRST ROUND 2019/20

Following their promotion to the National League North, Darlington had a really good first season in 2016/17 and finished a very creditable fifth, qualifying for the end-of-season play-offs. However, due to not having enough seats in their new ground at Blackwell Meadows, they weren't permitted to take part, which was a great shame.

Manager Martin Gray left to take over at York City during 2017/18 and was replaced by former player and FA Trophy winner Tommy Wright. Several players left and the club ended up finishing in the middle of the table.

Season 2018/19 was more of the same. I went to plenty of the home games, everything seemed flat and it came as no surprise to me when Wright was replaced by another former player in Alun Armstrong in time for the following season.

Under both Gray and Wright, Darlington had never had a decent FA Cup run, so it made a refreshing change to make it to the first round in 2019/20, a game that I attended with my wife Jen, and my PA Chris.

Due to my continuing health problems, after much discussion we decided to get a taxi from Darlington to Walsall the day before the game, and then come back the day after. This may seem a crazy, extravagant way to go to a football match that's well over 100 miles away, but given my needs, it was definitely the best option.

Anyway, prior to leaving for the match, the three of us decided to book a meal in Walsall's excellent hospitality suite. We weren't to be disappointed as it turned out to be really good value for money. The suite afforded a brilliant view of the pitch so we decided to watch the match from inside, given that it was a cold day.

The three of us witnessed an excellent performance from Darlington, who were playing against a team that were not only full-time (Darlington had been part-time since their relegation to the Northern League in 2012) but also two leagues above them.

As early as the 17th minute, Darlington were a goal up with Jamaican international Omar Holness scoring from the rebound after what was a brilliant save from Walsall keeper Jack Rose when he parried an original shot from the same player. The Quakers managed to hold on to their lead until the interval.

The hosts came more into the game in the second period and it came as no surprise when Caolan Lavery poked the ball home in the 86th minute. Worse was to follow when three minutes later the home side took the lead after the disappointing Darlington keeper Liam Connell punched the ball into his own net following a corner.

Connell had also been at fault for the home side's first goal when he had failed to hold on to the original shot prior to Lavery scoring.

Darlington poured men forward following Walsall's second goal and were rewarded seven minutes into injury time when former Middlesbrough midfielder Joe Wheatley bundled the ball home following a free kick from the now sadly deceased Osagi Bascome. This sent the hundreds of visiting supporters wild and gave Darlo a richly deserved replay.

Incidentally, both teams finished the game with ten men after Dan Scarr for Walsall and Darlington's Ben Hedley were sent off.

I have to say, after seeing that match, it was well worth the £400 taxi fare, plus two nights in a hotel.

Unfortunately, Darlington lost the replay 1-0 at Blackwell Meadows, a game that was featured on BT Sport.

I went to this game with Chris, but I had to leave at half-time due to the extreme cold.

Worse was to follow later that season when the campaign was curtailed because of the Covid-19 pandemic, with Alun Armstrong's men sitting in the middle of the league at the time the football was stopped.

6

The 2020s

SWINDON TOWN V DARLINGTON – FA CUP FIRST ROUND 2020/21

For the second season in a row, Darlington reached the first round of the FA Cup. On this occasion they were drawn a way to League One side Swindon Town. Unfortunately, no supporters were allowed to attend the match due to the ongoing Covid restrictions so, like several hundred Darlington fans, I watched the game live via the Swindon's live stream, at home with Jen.

We were lucky enough to see an excellent performance from Darlington. However, it could have been a different game if our keeper Jonathan Saltmer hadn't made brilliant saves from both Ellis Iandolo and Joel Grant. The save from the former was particularly impressive. Jen and I were celebrating in the 20th minute when we thought striker Luke Charman had given Darlo the lead, but the celebrations didn't last long as the goal was ruled out for offside. Former Bournemouth striker Brett Pitman could and maybe should have done better for the home side shortly after, but having been put clean through by Matt Smith he couldn't get his shot away and the chance was gone.

Former Newcastle striker Adam Campbell gave Darlo the lead in the 31st minute when a poor back header from Swindon's former Middlesbrough defender Jonathan Grounds left his keeper stranded, and Campbell took full advantage to score. This time Jen and I could celebrate and not end up being disappointed. Unfortunately, we were brought back down to earth when Pitman tapped the ball home following an excellent cross from Grant. This meant the scores were level at the interval.

The home side started the second half on the front foot and Jack Payne dithered on the ball instead of shooting and therefore lost the chance. Grant also fired over on the hour when he should have done better. Swindon were made to pay for those missed chances shortly after when the unfortunate Grounds, whom I have to say was very poor on the day, deflected the ball past his own keeper to give the Quakers the lead. The goal was later credited to Campbell. I sensed it was going to be our day after that.

Swindon's best chance came in the 80th minute when substitute Hallam Hope forced another save from Saltmer. With 15 minutes left Campbell almost scored again, but his shot was well saved by the Robins' keeper.

That turned out to be their last real chance and much to Jen's and my delight, Darlo were in the second round for the first time in many years. Saltmer and Campbell were brilliant and fully deserved to be on the winning side.

Darlo were drawn away to Bristol Rovers in the next round and unfortunately their run came to an end with a crushing 6-0 defeat. But the club made almost £100,000 from their FA Cup successes, money that is vital to a fan-owned club, which Darlington are.

Incidentally, just like the previous season, 2020/21 was curtailed in non-league football due to Covid. Darlington were in the bottom half of the league at the time, but they had played fewer matches than anyone else. At the time, I honestly thought that the club could have achieved something had they been allowed to continue playing. Unfortunately, it wasn't to be.